D1600166

Augustine and the Limits of Politics

Frank M. Covey, Jr.,
Loyola Lectures in Political Analysis
Thomas S. Engeman
General Editor

Our late colleague Richard S. Hartigan founded the Frank M. Covey, Jr., Lectures in Political Analysis to provide a continuing forum for the reanimation of political philosophy. The lectures are not narrowly constrained by a single topic nor do they favor a particular perspective. Their sole aim is to foster serious theoretical inquiry, with the expectation that this effort will contribute in essential ways to both human knowledge and political justice.

Augustine and the Limits
—— of Politics ——

Jean Bethke Elshtain

University of Notre Dame Press
NOTRE DAME, INDIANA

Copyright 1995 by University of Notre Dame Press
Notre Dame, Indiana, 46556
All Rights Reserved
Manufactured in the United States of America

Library of Congress Cataloging-in-Publication Data

Elshtain, Jean Bethke, 1941–
    Augustine and the limits of politics / by Jean Bethke Elshtain.
        p.   cm. — (Frank M. Covey, Jr. Loyola lectures in political analysis)
    Includes index.
    ISBN 0-268-00645-8 (alk. paper)
    1. Augustine, Saint, Bishop of Hippo—Contributions in relation of
Christianity to politics. 2. Christianity and politics. 3. Christianity and
politics—History of doctrines—Early church, ca. 30-600. I. Title.
II. Series.
BR1720.A9E57 1995   95-16515
261.7'092—dc20   CIP

The paper used in this publication meets the minimum requirements of the
American National Standard for Information Sciences—Permanence
of Paper for Printed Library Materials, ANSI Z39.48-1984.

To those who taught me well

Behold, and again see if you can. Certainly you love only the good, because the earth is good by the height of its mountains, the moderate elevation of its hills, and the evenness of its fields; and good is the farm that is pleasant and fertile; and good is the house that is arranged throughout in symmetrical proportions and is spacious and bright; and good are the animals, animate bodies; and good is the mild and salubrious air; and good is the food that is pleasant and conducive to health; and good is health without pains and weariness; and good is the countenance of man with regular features, a cheerful expression, and a glowing color; and good is the soul of a friend with the sweetness of concord and the fidelity of love; and good is the just man; and good are riches because they readily assist us; and good is the heaven with its own sun, moon, and stars; and good are the angels by their holy obedience; and good is the lecture that graciously instructs and suitably admonishes the listener; and good is the poem with its measured rhythm and the seriousness of its thoughts.

Augustine, De Trinitate

CONTENTS

A Village of the Mind

The usual cowardly caveats apply. I am not an Augustinian scholar. My Latin is sketchy and altogether inadequate to read Augustine in the original. I do not "keep up" with the continuous flow of Augustinian scholarship. That, I dare say, would be beyond the ken of any single human being, even one whose life was dedicated solely to the works of Augustine of Hippo. I discovered Augustine when I was eighteen years old and read a radically truncated version of his *Confessions*—although I didn't know enough to know that at the time. As I struggled with belief and unbelief, faith and skepticism, abandoning (so I then thought) my Lutheran beliefs and identity, I found I could not bid Augustine adieu. For one thing, I had only just become acquainted with him during that period of time when I had begun to put myself through ordeals of relentless interrogation of that past which was my own.

Convinced that I had left behind me once and for all Wittenberg and its general environs, I discovered, much to my surprise, that the rocky road I was traveling seemed to be heading south, in the general direction of Rome. How could that be? If Enlightenment was supposed to succeed, even defeat Faith, shouldn't I be pointed north toward Könisberg or west toward Paris? I took an intensive crash course on Kant, and then another, but I emerged not only unconvinced but unmoved. The air seemed awfully thin up there. And the Cartesian *cogito* made no sense to me at all. Having had polio as a child and given birth to my own first child at age nineteen, bodies loomed rather large in my scheme of things. As well, having fallen in love with Albert Camus (also at age eighteen), I had found an eloquent ally in my repudiation of rationalistic triumphalism and the repellent politics invited by "logical delirums," in Camus's words. I was too much a democrat and too aware of the human propensity to sin to believe that humans could create a perfect world of any sort on this fragile globe. Later I would learn to call my stance a recognition of the "noetic effects of sin," and, although I didn't have this phrase as a teenager, I had already been deeply imbued with, and defined by, the concept.

So I am, in a way, fated to wander the footpath that ambles from Wittenberg to Rome, not knowing whether I will ever see Rome; reverse direction and return to Wittenberg; or simply meander ongoingly in between, perhaps stopping along the way to take up lodgings in a village where the conversation is good, the neighbors friendly, the library well-stocked, the stirring words of "A Mighty Fortress Is Our God" emanate from the small Lutheran church, the bell from the Catholic church marks the passing of the day, the sounds of the Torah being read in the local synagogue float in the air, and rousing gospels from the black Baptist church beckon.

When I enter the village, it is "rock classics" night on the radio station and Elvis is singing "Don't Be Cruel." I see grandmothers on front stoops; hear a newborn baby's first cry; witness a funeral procession wending its way haltingly to the local cemetery, loathe to bid a loved one farewell. I observe boys and girls playing kick the can at dusk, hear dogs barking as night falls, and mothers and fathers reading bedtime stories to drowsy children. The notices in the town newspaper report that the book club is meeting at the Welch home to discuss this month's text— James Joyce's *The Dead*; that a well-known visiting theater troupe will perform Chekhov's *The Cherry Orchard* at the high school auditorium on Friday night; and that the movie theater, aptly named "The Lyric," is showing a series of Hollywood classics—

"The Man Who Shot Liberty Valance" is this week's feature. Frequenters of the local pub, The Town Tavern, are arguing politics and religion—the important things—well into the night.

Of course, this village no more exists than does Plato's far grander "city in speech" as designed for his *Republic*. But my village is a more liveable, because humbler, place. It has its boundaries, of course, but it extends hospitality to all strangers, wanderers, pilgrims, to the lost, the forlorn, the bold, and the timid. It is a rather simple place, this village of the mind, but it is a human landscape, a site within which beings such as ourselves enact daily the small gestures of kindness and trust and care and speaking out for fair treatment that are the stuff of lived life. Because that is not all that beings such as ourselves do, the village has its share of malicious gossip and backbiting and pettiness and scandal, but because people have to live and work together, none of this is codified into rival adversarial sides or camps. They understand what it means to tend to the quotidian. They understand forgiveness.

As with all villages, this one sends many of its sons and daughters out into the world, some never to return. A few of them do deeds the world calls 'great.' Most do not. Some are lost forever to the rapture of more exotic, forbidding, or violent places. But the village of the mind perdures. What is our business "within this common mortal life," Augustine asks and bids us ask ourselves. On the footpath that leads away from Wittenberg, as my travels draw me further from the boundaries of the village, I am never without company on the way. One of my companions is Augustine. This book is the story of an engagement, one *peregrinus* to, and with, another.

My thanks to Loyola University of Chicago for the opportunity to deliver the Covey Lectures, 1995. Thomas Engeman kept me on track and the Department of Political Science, Loyola, its faculty and students, were gracious hosts and engaged interlocutors. Over the years I have discussed Augustine with family, students, colleagues, friends, and Augustinian scholars. It would be impossible to disentangle all the strands of indebtedness but these are many and themselves testify to the exquisite sociality of our lives and the dense texture of friendship and amiability of which Augustine writes so eloquently.

Why Augustine? Why Now?

In his classic book *The Waning of the Middle Ages*, Johan Huizinga writes of the lurchings, portents, signs, dislocations, and spreading dis-ease that marked the closure of one era and the uneven and often violent birth of another.[1] Hannah Arendt, in the preface to her collection of essays *Between Past and Future*, describes our condition as that of living in a "gap" between past and future.[2] We are *zwischen den Zeiten*, she claims, between the times. Arendt was writing nearly thirty years ago, but, if anything, we sense with growing urgency that we are nearing the end of an era. Perhaps this can simply be attributed to the coming of a new millennium. We know from previous epochs that stepping over the boundary that separates one century from another sends a collective *frisson* through humankind, whether those who face the next hundred years with grandiose hopes or those who approach it with foreboding reservations. Many there are who are buoyant about our prospects. They write enthusiastically about a "third wave" of civilization that will overtake us, a time in the near future in which we will all greet one another happily in cyberspace and the world will be as one via electronic egalitarianism and populist technocracy. There are those who continue to toot the horns and ring the bells marking—rightly—the collapse of the Soviet Empire. But there are problems. There always are. Although 1989 by no means ushered in an era of peace and justice, the slogan "the enlargement of markets and democracy" is what now passes as a foreign policy for the United States. And yet . . . my sense is that, in the dark of the night, as dusk settles over the land and we stare at our television sets or take time to read the newspaper, we are plunged into a deepening gloom. Things were supposed to be better, different somehow, than this.

For what do we see when we look around? We see families imploding and crime exploding. Moral panics flourish. Liberal democracy is in trouble in America, the wise and the worried tell us, and many of us believe this to be true. Experts and ordinary citizens lament the growth of mistrust, cynicism, and scandal. Although a dwindling band of pundits and apologists insist that we are simply going through birth pangs en route to a more glorious and productive future, such reassurances ring increasingly hollow. By any standard of objective evidence, those who point to the growth of corrosive forms of isolation, boredom, and despair; to declining levels of involvement in politics; to the overall weakening of that world known as democratic civil society, have the better case. It is true that we brighten to tales of community, especially if the talk is soothing and doesn't demand very much from us. But when discussion turns to institutions and the need to sustain authoritative institutions of all kinds—and here I include families and churches and schools as well as governing bodies—attention withers and a certain sourness sets in. This bodes ill, for any ongoing way of life requires robust yet resilient institutions that embody and reflect, mediate and shape, our passions and our interests. As these overlapping associations of social life disappear or are stripped of legitimacy, a political and ethical wilderness spreads. People roam the prairie fixing on objects or policies or persons to excoriate or to celebrate, at least for a time, until some other enthusiasm or scandal sweeps over them. If we have lost the sturdiness and patience to sustain our society over the long haul, then our democracy, as a social world and a culture, is in trouble.

What can Augustine possibly have to say about any of this? Born in 354 in a provincial town in what is now Algeria; dying as Bishop of Hippo in North Africa in 430, what remains of Augustine are his vast works. After Augustine's death a full list of those works was compiled, and Possidius, who did the compiling, believed no single human being could ever hope to read them all, according to Peter Brown, Augustine's biographer. Brown also claims that Isidore of Seville "once wrote that if anyone told you he had read all the works of Augustine, he was a liar. From the time of his conversion to Catholic Christianity in 386 until his death in 430, Augustine wrote some 117 books."[3] That in and of itself would not recommend Augustine to us. But listen, if you will, to these words:

> The depraved and distorted hopes of men esteem human fortunes happy when the splendor of buildings is in evidence, and the collapse of souls is not noticed; when magnificent theatres are erected, and the foundations of virtue are undermined; when the madness of extravagance is glorified, and the works of mercy are scoffed at. . . .[4]

Or these:

> Who can adequately describe, or even imagine, the work of the Almighty? There is, first, this capacity for the good life, the ability to attain eternal felicity, by those arts which are called virtues, which are given solely by the grace of God in Christ to the children of the promise and of the kingdom. . . . Think of the wonderful inventions of clothing and building, the astounding achievements of human industry! Think of man's progress in agriculture and navigation; of the variety, in conception and accomplishment, man has shown in pottery, in sculpture, in painting; the marvels in theatrical spectacles, in which man's contrivances in design and production have excited wonder in the spectators and incredulity in the minds of those who heard of them. . . . Finally, the brilliant wit shown by philosophers and heretics in defending their very errors and falsehoods is something which beggars imagination![5]

Or:

> What tigress does not gently purr over her cubs, and subdue her fierceness to caress them? What kite, however solitary as he hovers over his prey, does not find a mate, build a nest, help to hatch

the eggs, rear the young birds, and, as we may say, preserve with the mother of his family a domestic society as peaceful as he can make it? How much more strongly is a human being drawn by the laws of his nature, so to speak, to enter upon a fellowship with all his fellow-men and to keep peace with them, as far as lies in him.[6]

Our poignant and powerful sociality brings us grief, yes, but also the most joyous of blessings. Augustine's childhood friend dies and his "heart grew sombre with grief."

> My own country became a torment and my own home a grotesque abode of misery. All that we had done together was now a grim ordeal without him. My eyes searched everywhere for him, but he was not there to be seen. I hated all the places we had known together, because he was not in them and they could no longer whisper to me "Here he comes!" as they would have done had he been alive but absent for a while. . . . Tears alone were sweet to me, for in my heart's desire they had taken the place of my friend.[7]

Who, then, is this complex man, this marvel of nature, as some have called him? Who is Augustine for us now? And what have the few words I have just noted—words of prophetic warning; marvel at the wondrous accomplishments of human beings, even in the service of error; appreciation of the tender-heartedness and familial concern of tigresses and vigilant male birds; sorrow at the loss of a friend—to do with political inquiry? That is, after all, the prompting and imperative that animates my engagement with Augustine and the limits of politics.

The Self at Stake

Perhaps a little dance of Augustine *sic et non* will bring him into clearer focus for us in order that we might grapple with him more robustly. In his wonderful biography, Peter Brown claims that Augustine has "come as near to us . . . as the vast gulf that separates a modern man from the culture and religion of the later empire can allow."[8] Brown has in mind, specifically, *The Confessions*. Let us focus, therefore, on Augustine and the self, in part because we late-twentieth-century humans are so preoccupied with ourselves. It would seem that if Augustine commends himself to us, it will be through the prism of the self, because he was certainly no liberal democrat; he didn't talk about a social contract; rights are not part of his political vocabulary; his understanding of authority is pretty much opaque to us, believing, as we do, that even persuasion is a form of imposition. But confession, so long as it is the individual talking about herself, *that* we sanction. Indeed, we now like to talk endlessly about the self. Is Augustine a kind of confessional forefather, then? This, I fear, would be a case of mistaken identity. For the self that is confessing in Augustine's great work bears almost no resemblance to those selves that shamelessly parade their secrets on American television any day of the week. One is struck by the harshness, the meanness, and the utter predictability of many of these displays, as well as the aggressive ways in which confession and scandal have become weapons of war and instruments of pitiless assault against family and friends and that obscure enemy, Society, the world at large. One is saddened by the thinness of the selves put on display. There is little density and texture, all the marvels that are the subject of Book X of *The Confessions*, an evocation of memory unsurpassed in Western literature save, perhaps, in the works of Proust.

Augustine confesses what he knows and what he does not know. He does know the world isn't boundlessly subjectivist; it does not revolve around what my mother calls "me, myself, and I."

> My love of you, o Lord, is not some vague feeling; it is positive and certain. . . . But what do I love when I love my God? Not material beauty or beauty of a temporal order; not the brilliance of earthly light, so welcome to our eyes; not the sweet melody of harmony and song; not the fragrance of flowers, perfumes, and spices; not manna or honey; not limbs such as the body delights to embrace. It is not

these that I love when I love my God. And yet, when I love him, it is true that I love a light of a certain kind, a voice, a perfume, a food, an embrace; but they are of the kind that I love in my inner self, when my soul is bathed in light that is not bound by space; when it listens to sound that never dies away; when it breathes fragrance that is not borne away on the wind; when it tastes food that is never consumed by the eating; when it clings to an embrace from which it is not severed by fulfillment of desire. This is what I love when I love my God.[9]

This love frames other loves. It draws Augustine out of himself and the vortex of immediacy. It affords him the grandeur of a potent yet restrained lyricism that never grows sentimental, because it is borne out and up, so to speak, and it never loses its object, never becomes formless. When one loves only one's self, the self grows thin and flattens out; it reduces to a defensive point of order or oozes indiscriminately into a general sociological morass. If every external point of reference is lost, we lose our very selves. But we do not want to hear this. For the most part, I doubt that we believe it.

We don't believe it because we have turned the loss of a confessing self who is drawn out of the self in order to be for others into an all-consuming self, an expressivist exhibition. Such self-consumed selves when they appear in public are then melded together, so to speak, forming a dense wall of immanence where every reference point is anthropocentric. This is analogous to the isolation people experience in totalitarian regimes, according to Hannah Arendt, where privation is followed by, indeed is the precondition for, the forging of an iron band of coercion. All plurality—all the space between people—is forfeit. Of course, we confront nothing so dire. But how much room is left, I wonder—how much space between people—so that selves might recognize one another in their distinctiveness, yet come together in friendship or solidarity, perhaps because they jointly "sigh" or "yearn" for that which is foreshadowed in the *civitas terrena*? There is no room for sighing or wonder or shame or reticence or praise in our crass spectacles of publicity. We need others, our popular culture suggests, as an addict needs a drink or a weapon needs a target.

And yet it is Augustine who now falls under a cloud of clinical suspicion. One reads his *Confessions*. He spends a lot of time talking about loving God and finding, or collecting, a self; about the evils of the flesh ("hissing cauldron of lust" in one memorable phrase) and what counts as an excess of *curiositas*. He takes to task his contemporaries for their gullibility and the folly of their faith in astrologers and soothsayers. That no doubt makes some among our contemporaries cross. Walk into any bookstore in America today and if you want to be gulled and offered code books to read the signs and predict your fate, or embrace half-baked theories promoted by people with remedies in their rucksacks and potions in their pockets, you will have no difficulty consuming remedies and taking cures and nostrums to your heart's delight. What does Augustine offer by contrast? No cure for one's ills. Rather, a dauntingly complex philosophic discourse *about* our ills, about the nature of memory itself, and about the distinction between literal, allegorical, and figurative meaning as we read and interpret texts, including Scripture. What has this to do with coming clean about personal addiction or love affairs with reckless men or hating your mother or wanting to kill your father? What indeed.

Augustine's *Confessions* have long been a stumbling block to American liberal theology. When Charles Norris Cochrane penned his classic *Christianity and Classical Culture*, published in 1957, he argued that "modern liberal theology apparently finds Augustine almost wholly unintelligible." He cites one A. C. MacGiffert, who wrote *A History of Christian Thought*, as typical: "In his doctrine of God and man and sin and grace, the curious combination of mystic piety, Neoplatonic philosophy, Manichean dualism, Christian tradition, strained exegesis, rigorous logic and glaring inconsistencies born of religious instincts and moral needs, can hardly be matched in the history of human

thought."[10] American humanism had "no hesitation in denounc-
ing" Augustine, Cochrane continues, for his supposed slighting
of the intellect and his willful obscurantism. William James lo-
cates Augustine as a classical example of "the discordant personality," waxing eloquent about "his half-pagan, half-Christian
bringing-up at Carthage, his emigration to Rome and Milan,
his adoption of Manicheism and subsequent scepticism, and his
restless search for truth and purity of life. . . ." Then comes the
famous moment, the voice in the garden saying "*tolle, lege*" and
Augustine's "inner storm" is laid to rest, or so James suggests. For
James, what Augustine offers to later generations is an unsurpassed account of the trouble of "having a divided self."[11] Take
note that it is Augustine's "divided self," not an account of that
division which simply *is* the human condition after the Fall and
before the end-time, that gap when humanity is squeezed in
temporality, marked by finitude, and unable to cast off the noetic
effects of sin.

Traveling down the path sketched earlier by James, but without
his urgency and insight, subsequent psychological commentators
set up Augustine's as the story of a diseased psyche. Augustine's
mother, the formidable Monica, looms rather large, to say the
least; the "two cities" become subjectivized as unresolved parts of
Augustine's psyche; *mater ecclesia* is the overbearing mother he
finally permits himself to be engulfed by, on and on. As Cochrane
rightly notes, the overriding passion of Augustine's life—the passion for truth—is lost or reduced to the neurotic obsession of a
brilliant but peculiar man. Paul Rigby, in an essay on "Paul
Ricoeur, Freudianism, and Augustine's *Confessions*," argues that *The
Confessions* as written are "no longer credible to modernity," for we
must "first make a detour through the unconscious to come to
true self-knowledge." Our age "requires a Freudian interpretation" of a text as "personal" as *The Confessions*.[12] This Freudian
moment is a necessarily deconstructive one in any modern appropriation of a classical religious text if that text is to be credible to

our age. Rigby tries not to be reductionistic and he repudiates such representations as those of David Bakan, who finds the Oedipal elements in Augustine's story "patent" and characterizes Monica as a "frigid hypermoral woman concealing incestuous gratification in story scenes."[13]

Reading this, I wondered what "story scenes" Bakan might have in mind. Could it be this moment, from Book IX of *The Confessions*, when Augustine describes the death of Monica and her courage in telling her son that he should bury her there, in Ostia, far from her native land. "It does not matter where you bury my body. Do not let that worry you! All I ask of you is that, wherever you may be, you should remember me at the altar of the Lord."[14] She absolves her son of the traditional requirement that one be interred in the soil of one's native land. For she is a Christian. God will know where to find her. Augustine's friends marvel at her courage. She wants no special monument or grave. But Augustine (addressing God) hopes that those who "read this book" will

> remember Monica, your servant, at your altar and with her Patricius, her husband, who died before her, by whose bodies you brought me into this life, though how it was I do not know. With pious hearts let them remember those who were not only my parents in this light that fails, but were also my brother and sister, subject to you, our Father, in our Catholic mother the Church, and will be my fellow citizens in the eternal Jerusalem for which your people sigh throughout their pilgrimage, from the time when they set out until the time when they return to you. So it shall be that the last request that my mother made to me shall be granted in the prayers of the many who read my confessions more fully than in mine alone.[15]

To me these are the appropriate words of a loving son to a beloved mother; an embodiment of classical *pietas*.

Rigby's relative hermeneutical generosity in this matter is too much for one Donald Capps to bear. He responds with a broadside on "Augustine as Narcissist." He agrees that a "modern reading of *The Confessions* must include a Freudian deconstruction that cannot finally be set aside once introduced." (He accuses Rigby of having done this.) For Augustine's "account of his interpersonal relationships, especially involving his mother, evokes the suspicion of the modern reader, and such suspicion cannot be expunged from any 'higher' reading of the text."[16] Notice the heavy burden Capps bears: he *must* be "suspicious." He will not permit anyone to slip through the net of his hermeneutics of suspicion. And he cites a slew of other folks who detect narcissism in *The Confessions*. For Augustine seems preoccupied with himself in a number of ways and has an "immature attitude toward sexuality."[17]

So the real, indeed, the *only* question, for Capps is: should the Oedipal issues predominate in interpreting Augustine, or is narcissism the key to the whole matter? Narcissism wins the day, being defined by (1) resistance to the claims of others, (2) manipulation of the impressions they make on other persons, (3) a shallow emotional life, and (4) resistance to acknowledging their finitude. Augustine's way out is "the powerfully idealized parental image"—that's God, in case the reader hadn't guessed. The person crafting this harsh reductio offers a remarkably thin account, and the lack of textual evidence to back up the clinical label of Augustine as narcissist is stunning.

For *The Confessions* is, among the many things that it is, a story of the claims of others on the self—the claims of friendship and *pietas* toward elders and respect for the *auctoritas* of great mentors like St. Ambrose. It is a story of a man "becoming a question to himself" and struggling with the immediacy of desire, leading to a discernment that if the self lives only in the immediacy of desire, then others are simply grist for one's mill; then the claims of others have no authentic space within which to emerge. The woman with whom Augustine had been living in a monogamous relationship is torn from his side—he cannot marry her given the impediments his provincial and hence uncertain social class and fortunes and, yes, his mother's strenuous objections, presented—and "this was a blow which crushed my heart to bleeding, because I loved her dearly." But rather than making a "proper marriage," as his mother had hoped, he converts, and he and his closest friends decide to live a holy life together. That lust and concupiscence were problems for him in all this is true but precisely because the body was good, created by God, meant to be loved and cherished. Indeed, Augustine explicitly repudiates the narcissistic self-absorption of those caught in the grip of a lust to dominate, what Romand Coles calls an "ontology of conceit" and mastery.[18] Rejecting the dominant motif of classical antiquity—the male subject as a hunter, one who pursues and traps and controls his prey; one who, in order to be a self, must be a self that dominates others—Augustine shifts the ontology of the self, relocates the self in a transformed understanding, and moves toward a self that is no longer dominated by a need to dominate, nor bound by the immediacy of desire.

The question isn't so much how to control an old self, but how to bring a transformed one into being. The effects are immediate; that is, certain performative requirements flow from this shift in the *gravamen* of the self. A new community of believers and friends, a community united by *caritas* and the explicit repudiation of a role Augustine had come to see as manipulative of others, the identity of rhetor and teacher of rhetoric, is complete. Indeed, Augustine had earlier taken his leave of the Manichees, in part because they "lapse into pride" and their "conceit soars like a bird" when they believe, wrongly, that they can calculate human events with precision in the way a legitimate astronomer can calculate the day and hour of an eclipse.

Against "Self-Esteem"

Augustine enters the lists directly with his sustained critique of self-esteem, and if the contemporary shoe fits, wear it, he would no doubt tell us. What is at stake here? For Augustine, self-esteem—a high regard for oneself where one is the sole estima-

tor or appraiser of the self—is the disease, not the cure. "I was inflated with self-esteem, which made me think myself a great
man,"[19] he writes and in another formulation describes being full
of "self-esteem" as "a punishment of my own making."[20] He
ironically suggests that the study of rhetoric and the quest for
worldly success it generates makes one fret more about a mispro-
nunciation of the word for a human being than about the concrete human being himself or herself.[21] How anyone can derive
narcissism from this is a mystery if one cares at all about persuasive evidence and compelling argument. But that isn't what is
going on in these *reductio* hit and runs, is it? Rather, in and from
contemporary conceit, we believe we can tear everything down
that others have built; that we can reduce lives to formulae; that
we can explain away any claims the past may make on us; that we,
then, can be left to ourselves. But if we care about the self and
what we have made, or are making, of selves in late modernity,
Augustine cannot be turned into a medical specimen and placed
on the shelf featuring famous neurotics of the past quite so
quickly.

His self is a story of the transformation of feeling. It is not
about attaining a moment of clairvoyance or perfect understanding that persists as a way of knowing in the world. Augustine
warns against such overreach. "Whoever thinks that in this mortal life a man may so disperse the mists of bodily and carnal
imaginings as to possess the unclouded light of changeless truth,
and cleave to it with the unswerving constancy of a spirit wholly
estranged from the common ways of life—he understands neither what he seeks, nor who he is who seeks it."[22] If we cannot
attain perfection, what, then, is the drama of confession and *con-
versio*? Where does it tend?

Augustine offers multiple metaphors and analogies and sim-
iles to help his reader understand and to profess the God that, in
and through confessing, helped him to find his very self. His
once scattered self is gathered together. His heart has ears that are
ready to listen; whisper into "my heart's ears," he pleads to the

Lord. By watching babies he determines that they are always in a world of flawed interpretation. The baby makes a sign to show meaning, but it is not perfectly understood. The baby grows cross and takes revenge by bursting into tears. Augustine learns much from watching babies and from what women "have to tell" as a result of their tending to babies. He discerns that we call children "innocent" only because they lack the power to do harm. Yet he notices a baby grow "livid" as it watches another baby nurse. "I have myself seen jealousy in a baby and know what it means."[23]

Once boyhood begins and with it the "power of speech," the child learns that there is a kind of universal language of features, tones, expressions, eye movements and takes a further step into the "stormy life of human society." He—that boy called Augustine—dreads the punitive punishment of schoolmasters and yet he knows he would not have studied had he not been compelled. But he concludes, nonetheless, that we learn better in a free spirit of curiosity than from under a thunderstorm of fear and compulsion. The conventions of language are mastered; the sins and scandals of youth enacted. He is gripped by frenzies of lust, wanting only to love and to be loved. He participates in stealing pears for the pleasure of doing a forbidden thing and for friendship's sake. He wasn't hungry. He loved the wrong things. His desire tended in directions that further tore at his soul and fragmented his self. He discovers Cicero and Hortensius and his heart begins to throb with a "bewildering passion" for wisdom. Philosophy sets him aflame. He is put off, however, by Scripture, with its low rhetoric, its humble characters, its inelegant prose, its God who goes through a human life even unto an ignominious death. Remember: "I was inflated with self-esteem, which made me think myself a great man."[24]

But light starts to dawn. He discerns distinctions between conventional understandings of justice and God's true underlying justice; he observes the desecration of relationships through lust and domination; he can "make no progress" with Manichean theories concerning evil, including its categories of the elect pure and the great lot of the impure and its inability to account coherently for the phenomenon of evil. Struggling to reach God, he remained "all words" and all at sea about God's nature. The story continues and it is a story of challenge, discovery, advances in reason and understanding, disappointments with the high and mighty, the recognition of greater truths among those humbler texts of Scripture, backsliding and doubt. He mocks himself, cheeks puffed up with pride, because he learns ten Aristotelian categories and can reduce everything that exists to these categories, or so he believes for a time.

He was living behind his own back, so to speak, his "heart" was "shut away," but it could not hide and, finally, having given up his philosophical materialism and moved to face straight on the problem of evil which he had once, in Manichean fashion, construed as an actual bodily substance, an essentialist category of impure things by contrast to the pure, the scales fall from his eyes. The Manichean attempt to de-Judaize the Church is wrong; the derivation of evil from alternative types of substances is incoherent; the language of Scripture is available to all and open for figurative interpretation. One can make progress in it. Unlike the Manichees, Christians need not make promises of scientific proof for every point of doctrine, for the Christian understands that we are too weak to discover all the truth by reason alone. We need the authority of sacred books; we need a community of interlocutors; we require a dialogue with ourselves and our buffeted hearts; we need the practices and saving presences of a community; we come to understand that God is not a bodily substance scattered throughout the material world, with more of him in an elephant and less in an earthworm; evil is not a countersubstance similarly dispersed and in opposition.

Augustine's heart goes into labor and gives birth to humility. Evil is no power unto itself; it is a privation. It is my will—for "I knew I had a will"—I will therefore I am. I know I am capable of willing and nilling; I know as well that that which I would do, I do not, for the will is weak and imperfect. The fault, dear Brutus, lies not in the stars but in ourselves that we are underlings, says Cassius in Shakespeare's *Julius Caesar*. The fault, dear reader, Augustine tells us, lies not in evil demiurges and their tainted representatives in the world, but in one's divided will. This recognition opens up a paradoxical freedom, lays the basis for a transformed self; the heart's labors bring forth new life.

As an old man, having been bishop of Hippo for thirty-nine years, having survived assassination attempts and troubles of all sorts, knowing the Vandals are closing in on his city and all may well be lost, including the vast collection of his own works, he retreats to his study, re-reading his many works at night, working at his desk as bishop during the day. Brown tells us that Augustine "wanted to see his works as a whole, that they might be read, in future, by men who had reached the same certainty as himself, by mature Catholic Christians."[25] Looking back on his *Confessions*, the dying man writes: "As for me, they still move me, when I read them now, as they moved me when I first wrote them."[26] To be unmoved by *The Confessions*, to see in them only feed for the clinical grinder; only evidence of a solidification of the triumph of Western logocentricism, is to have a heart of stone and a head of brick. Indeed, this story embodies a profound and radical shift away from the dominant heroic ethic of the antique world. Here Augustine offers us a transformed self that will people the new city, an *altera civitas*, a city that has broken with the war-fighting fortress of old. By condemning "every tendency toward a view of personhood as 'self ownership' and of ownership itself as unrestricted freedom within one's own domain," Augustine gives birth to a new set of possibilities.[27] The self judges, acts, wills, and nills, but it can never attain perfection; omniscience is God's alone. Hence, Augustine's ease at spelling out a hermeneutic theory of polysemy and multiple interpretations. Why should this surprise us, he asks, for we grasp diverse truths in different ways at different points, insofar as we are able. All of this is fairly common knowledge—widely accepted among Augustinian scholars.

But my primary purpose at this juncture is to pound nails in the coffin of reckless labeling, particularly use of the clinical term narcissism, once and for all.[28] To this end, let's take up the question of *identity*, another way we have devised to talk nonstop about ourselves. As currently deployed, identity often does gesture toward others, most often others we think of as being like ourselves, as in contemporary *identity politics*. We use sameness within the group to shore up claims of difference against some other (putatively) homogeneous group. This is a dubious activity for many reasons. But Augustine advances a fascinating argument against the obliteration of distinctiveness by those who favor absolutizing a principle of difference. Those who promote this latter agenda insist that difference goes "all the way down," that one is *at one* with oneself—whether one's ethnicity, color, sexual identity, gender, and that this constitutes the *selfsame self*, the *me* that demands that the world recognize her. In his discussion of the selfsame, Augustine undercuts decisively arguments launched from these standpoints of essentialism or radically subjectivist expressivism.

Picture this. The bishop is speaking to his flock, offering Homilies on the Psalms. Today he takes up Psalm 121: The Ecstasy of Love. "Do you wish to see the quality of love? See where it leads." He warns about being too tied to earthly loves and not drawn forth, not able to soar, to free oneself from the affections of this world. But primarily he wants to explain how the human being is not and never can be the Selfsame. We can partake of the heavenly Jerusalem. We can gaze with our minds and lift them up to contemplate the Selfsame. What is the Selfsame? "That which exists always in the same way, which is not now one thing and again something else." But this is never true of our mutability and the variety of temporal things. Given these, we cannot "know the meaning of the Selfsame." Notice how the present moment is gone as soon as we remark on it. Nothing abides forever. "Man's mind, called rational, is changeable, never the same. Sometimes it wishes, sometimes it does not wish; sometimes it knows; sometimes it does not know; sometimes it remembers and sometimes it forgets. No one has, therefore, Selfsameness from himself."[29] The proud man, the self-absorbed man, simply refuses to partake of the Selfsame, for that would mean getting out of himself and acknowledging his own incompleteness. Instead, he "wishes to be the origin of himself."

But this cannot be. Without love, without charity, without Jerusalem, the City "whose partaking is in the Selfsame," the self is caught in a whirlpool of its own devising, and it spins further and further away—from self, from neighbor, from engagement with the created world, and from the Selfsame. For Augustine, many of our modern forms of identity triumphalism would be nothing less than a repudiation of the Selfsame as a transcendent principle and a grasping at the self as its own principle of being. In this way, as Václav Havel noted recently, we forget that we are not God. Havel writes:

> The relativization of all moral norms, the crisis of authority, the re-
> duction of life to the pursuit of immediate material gain without
> regard for its general consequences—the very things Western
> democracy is most criticized for—do not originate in democracy
> but in that which modern man has lost: his transcendental anchor,
> and along with it the only genuine source of his responsibility and
> self-respect. . . . Given its fatal incorrigibility, humanity probably
> will have to go through many more Rwandas and Chernobyls be-
> fore it understands how unbelievably shortsighted a human being
> can be who has forgotten that he is not God.[30]

That is because we aspire to *constitute* ourselves as the Self-same, forgetting that we *only partake* of That Which Is the Same Yesterday, Today, and Tomorrow. In thus forgetting, and it is no innocent forgetting, we forge forth as the principle of our own being, to mow down whatever stands in our way. Believing as we yet do, despite the demise of the totalitarian utopias of the twentieth century, in the dialectic of master/slave and the tele-ology of violence those utopias preached, we persist in constru-

ing the world as one of power *über alles*. The only question is
who will win and who will lose; who winds up at the top of the
heap; who gets sent down. We have sown the wind of envy and
resentment and we are reaping the whirlwind. This Augustine
would understand and he would try to "twinkle out a sermon"
for us on the real joys of human life, our capacity for surprise
and delight and love and yearning, for it is "yearning," he tells
us, "that makes the heart deep."[31] But we cannot yearn if we
have made ourselves the ground of our own Being. From an
anthropocentric presumption of the Selfsame, no open hearted
action nor loving dialogue can come, only the insistencies of a
clamorous, triumphalist self, full of demands, shorn of pity,
incapable of critical self-examination, disdainful of the only solidarity possible on our torn and tattered globe, that fragile communion the Czech philosopher Jan Patočka called "the solidarity
of the shattered."

2

The Earthly City and Its
Discontents

Augustine is usually numbered among the pessimists. I'm sure many readers remember being taught Augustine in this way. Political Augustinianism belonged with Machiavellianism and Hobbesianism as a way of looking at the world that stressed evil, cruelty, violence, and a concomitant need for order, coercion, punishment, and the occasional war. Of course, one didn't actually read Augustine so much as Augustine-fragments culled from the 'political' bits in *The City of God*. Perhaps a chunk from Book I, chapter 1, on "the city of this world, a city which aims at dominion, which holds nations in enslavement, but is itself dominated by that very lust of domination."[1] Book II, chapter 21 was helpful on Augustine's alternative to Cicero's judgment (according to Scipio) of the Roman commonwealth. Book XV, chapter 1, traced the lines of descent of the "two cities, speaking allegorically"; Book XIX, chapter 14, could be mined for a few precepts about the interests government should serve; chapter 15 made an argument against slavery "by nature"; and chapter 21, in which Scipio's definition of a commonwealth as advanced by Cicero makes a second appearance, also seemed pertinent. Book XIX was usually lodged as the key political text, containing what political theorists found relevant, not, of course, the debate on "Supreme Good and Evil" in chapter 1, but chapter 7 that spoke of "the misery of war even when just," as well as the most frequently excerpted chapters 14, 15, and 16, deployed in order to demonstrate that Augustine recognized a connection between the peace and good of the household in relation to the city, or to earthly dominion more grandly defined. That, plus his rather scathing comment that what pirates do with one boat, Romans do with a navy, but the one is called brigandage while the other is named Empire, and the student would have her quick intake of Augustine Lite.

Called upon to give a lecture on Augustine for a course I took over about a month into a spring term—the year was 1972, the regular professor had taken ill suddenly, and the university in question wanted an inexpensive replacement (in other words, a graduate student)—I found that the reading list included Augustine Lite with the usual excerpts rounded up. I recall well the day I was to teach Augustine: one such session was reserved on the syllabus. It was a frigid morning during a particularly nasty winter in the Northeast. The class met at 8 A.M. Most of the students worked; indeed, some came directly to class from their night jobs.

My night job was getting up with children and, as well, I faced over an hour's drive in subzero weather in a Volkswagen mini-van with no functioning heater in order to get to class. No one was in a particularly jaunty mood. I had quickly crammed a bit of secondary reading—there had been no time to read even an abridged version of *The City of God*, and *The Confessions*, or so I had been taught, had nothing to do with politics. I decided to offer up a few bits of instant wisdom on Political Augustinianism. I called it a "way of looking at the world" and it went like this—I can be rather precise because I managed to dig out my old notes:

(1) Pessimism. Augustine does not view political order as an agency for human progress. He is extremely skeptical about the possibility that politics holds out hope for human improvement or the unfolding of the fullness of human virtue. Is not man a creature characterized by perversity of the will, plagued by fleeting desires, prone to

sin, error, and perverse actions? Not too much can be expected from him.

(2) Evil is real. Man cannot be reformed.

(3) Augustine has a "tough-minded-realistic view of power." He sees power as the result of attempts to dominate. Power is not natural. It is devised by man. Power cannot be escaped; it can only be restrained.

(4) Authority must be treated with deference and respect but there is nothing inherently legitimate about it. It is a symptom of the fact that human beings do not spontaneously treat one another with love and affection.

I then asked the students: Even though political Augustinianism is not particularly attractive to us, might it not say something true about the human condition nonetheless? To be honest, I can't remember what followed. I do recall going over the nature of the two cities as formed by two loves, but as not having an "exact equivalent in this world." There are aspects of both cities in the life of this world, I claimed. The Church is not the heavenly city but prefigures it. For the Church itself is not perfect. It, too, uses powers of compulsion and control, although this is a tragic necessity, not something to celebrate or encourage. In theory, the Church can accommodate everyone and anyone: it is universalistic in principle.

The earthly city, I continued, is marked by the killing of Abel by Cain. Although violence is endemic to this city, it may promote a minimalist notion of the good, certainly better than a remorseless war of all against all. Earthly peace, though imperfect, is much to be desired. Because the political order is characterized by violence, regeneration cannot come from it: it cannot be a generative force from itself. Christians, however, can use the political order because it introduces regularity into social relations and thus helps to make possible the life of the Church.

The heavenly city, I told the by now no doubt dozing students, is important as Augustine's analysis of the earthly city makes sense only in relation to it. Condemning Roman imperialism (for the Roman *imperium* is not a genuine community, only an illusory community of coercion and force), Augustine offers an image of a city united by a shared love, one in which relations are free from earthly coercion. I ended with the question of evil. Why does God permit it to exist, to play a significant role in human life? For things are not randomly arranged. God is the creator; God brought *ordo* or order into being. Here I notice in my notes that I made a big mistake. I claimed that evil was ineradicable, for it was "brought into existence by God and can be removed only by Him." Where I derived this idea, I cannot be sure but I probably owe a public apology to those seventeen or so souls gathered on a Thursday morning in Boston over twenty years ago. Evil isn't God's doing, a point to which we will return in detail in chapter 4.

I concluded all those years ago by assaying what happens when one tries to make Augustine fit into the canon of Western political thought. This emerges mostly as a series of perorations on why Augustine is not a central figure for most political theorists. He does not believe living in political society transforms or completes our natures. He dissents from strong conceptions of justice. There is a rough and ready justice, to be sure, even in robber bands, but earthly justice is often little more than a principle of retribution as well as an imperfect sign of our sociality—it doesn't touch on the really important stuff.

And what is that? Here things got interesting, at least for me. I noted that Augustine criticizes Cicero's definition of a *respublica* as an association based on common agreement concerning right and on shared interests. Within the terms of this definition, Rome was never a true commonwealth. But Cicero's definition itself is wanting. A people is a gathering or multitude of rational beings united in fellowship by sharing a common love of the same things. Using such a definition, we can not only define what a society is, but we can also determine what it is that people hold dear. In proper graduate student in political theory fashion, I called Augustine's definition both "normative"—it allows us to evaluate the quality of contrasting societies—and "analytic"—it gives us a means of analyzing actual values sought and realized.[2]

Because *consensus* or *conflict* theory was much in the air then—rather like the *liberalism* and *communitarian* debate is now—I felt obliged to wade into that dispute and argued that Augustine didn't really belong in either camp. To be sure, communities are held together by what they hold dear. There is an affective aspect to it. Christians aspire to a community based on a brotherhood and sisterhood of belief. But most would consider this a- or anti-political. And there it ended—for the students but not for me.

I didn't particularly relish what I had done that day—having been forced to collect my thoughts under pressure of time and the constraints flowing from the nature and structure of a course syllabus I had not designed. I promised myself I would spend more time with Augustine. This chapter is, in part, a story of Augustine, my companion in a variety of modes of exploration, on that footpath leading out from Wittenberg and into those very peculiar villages we call universities. Over the years I took up public and private, war and peace, justice and that love of God and love of neighbor Augustine insists must be the basis of earthly life. Each encounter yielded more questions, a deepening astonishment at the apparent boundlessness of Augustine's vast curiosity, and dissatisfactions with my own take on things, for I was never sure I had quite gotten it right.

Why? Because Augustine's categories are not simple and do not comport with those most familiar to us in late-twentieth-century liberal political life. Indeed, the late George Armstrong Kelly proclaimed in 1984 that "in fair weather or foul, the Augustinian theory has little appeal for liberal society."[3] For example: Augustine's *civitas* is not a state; nor is it really a *respublica*. But if one calls it, simply, a *society*, one loses the attention and interest of political theorists, for society is what anthropologists and sociologists study unless, of course, it is *civil society* and then the reference point is either Hegel or the contemporary debate, much indebted to political thinkers and actors in Central Eastern Europe.[4] These problems are further compounded by the fact that there are so many Augustines—the pessimistic Augustine, already noted; the pluralist Augustine; the romantic Augustine; the reactionary Augustine; the sexist Augustine; the anti-sexist Augustine; even a sort of proto-socialist Augustine. It is altogether too easy to slice off one chunk of Augustine and turn that piece into the *real* Augustine or the only Augustine worth salvaging. But let us perservere nonetheless.

Augustine: The Plot Thickens

In a period of soul-searching following completion of graduate school comprehensive examinations, I returned to Augustine's *Confessions* and emerged both awed and moved. But I really hadn't the faintest idea what this had to do with political theory. *The City of God*, of course, was another story, so I waded back into it as part of my consideration of the public and the private in Western political thought. Even trying to place Augustine within a private/public prism was bound to do him an injustice. I began to conjure with the ways his work intruded, impinged, pushed beyond the boundaries, and crashed through the categories political theorists work with. Peter Brown suggests that *The City of God* is such a difficult book, and such an easy text to ignore, because it is huge; it is a narrative treating literally hundreds of issues and controversies, but in ways that do not lend themselves to stipulative definitions and readily codified formulae; and, perhaps most important, it has nothing whatever to do with what Brown calls the "Rational Myth of the State," the metaphor on which classical political theory from

> the seventeenth century onwards, was based. . . . By myth I mean the habit of extrapolating certain features of experience, isolating them, in abstraction or by imagining an original state in which only those elements were operative, and using the pellucid myth thus created as

a means of explaining what should happen today. The tendency, therefore, was to extrapolate a rational man; to imagine how reason, and a necessity assessed by reason, would lead him to found a state; and to derive from this 'mythical' rational act of choice a valid, rational reason for obeying, or reforming, the state as it now is.[5]

We moderns tend to presuppose a free-standing individual and then to posit a state that we call sovereign. What connects the individual to the state is a series of reciprocal rights and obligations. The state is the senior partner, of course, and can, if it desires, call most of the shots. The individual can proclaim rights but also has obligations. There isn't very much in-between. We know, of course, that there is lots of other stuff, but it goes unmentioned, untheorized, if you will.

Moving through *The City of God* with this myth of the individual and the state in my mind, but lodged there quite insecurely because I never quite got it—this story of the self and the state, for the world was so much denser, thicker, richer, and more complex than social contract metaphors and tales of rights and obligations allowed—I took up the distinction between the household and the *polis*, or the private and the public, because Aristotle had put that on the agenda explicitly and because feminists were vigorously proclaiming that the "private was the public" *tout court*, and that didn't seem quite right to me either.

It was hard not to get distracted in going through Augustine. His account of a naturalistic morality written on the hearts of sentient creatures. His critique of classical philosophy, much of it quite witty, including his unpacking of the Stoic quest for happiness and solace which culminates in suicide. The great stuff on war and peace. The discussion of languages and the ways they divide and unite us. The tongue as an instrument of domination. The emphasis on human freedom; we have free will; we can cleave to God (like the good angels, but in our own flawed human way) or turn away. But we must choose. His radical reconstruction of justice and injustice. His insistence that no one is evil by nature. Nor are we political by nature, although we are by nature social. Moreover, no man has natural dominion over his fellow men. And, of course, his powerful story of the two cities and the earthly pilgrimage of those who would be citizens in the City of God but were, at best, fitful members of the earthly city. This was tethered to the sobering material on the rising and falling of cultures, even great empires. As George Kelly observes: "St. Augustine wrote his greatest work not only to show that we are agents of some ultimate design toward which reason draws us while leaving us unsatisfied at the portals of faith but to diminish our expectations of the millennium and to cast back these disappointments on our ongoing earthly performance especially our political ones."[6]

Taken together, these insights led to the unmistakable conclusion that Augustine was subversive, shifting the center of earthly gravity away from the political order to the "solid rock" of the *civitas Dei* on pilgrimage. The Church, although not the precise referent for this City of God must, nevertheless, be an authoritative institution, one that gathers together, in its wayfaring, citizens from all races, all tongues, both sexes, and unites them into the commonality of a single but dispersed pilgrim band. Their particularity is preserved—the diversity of customs, laws, and traditions not only need not but cannot be overturned in the name of a uniform Christian society. For God loves contrasts and differences. The earthly peace preserved by these orders, though sadly wanting with reference to the ultimate, is the best that creatures in the penultimate can aspire to. Earthly peace may be illusory but it should be cherished nonetheless. The major disturbers of the peace are often those who claim to be upholding it—the great empires and great men—overtaken by a lust of sovereign dominion which disturbs and consumes the human race with frightful ills. Don't tell me so-and-so was great because he assaults and consumes the human race with his insatiable quest for earthly riches and glory, Augustine chides. This was a rich and diverse repast: how to pare it down to size in order to explicate the public and the private?

I decided to begin with Wittgenstein, having become intrigued by the fact that *The City of God* "was one of the very few books visible in Wittgenstein's sparsely decorated rooms at Cambridge and that he cited and referred to [it] often."[7] The answer to Wittgenstein's love affair with Augustine lay in the richness of Augustine's complex philosophy of language in which meaning played a central role. As well, language—its multiple possibilities of interpretation and its dispersion and difference—helps to account for the irremediable murkiness of human affairs. The relationship of words to the stuff of the world is, at best, imprecise—always riddled with ambivalence and ambiguity. Our understanding and our actions must always be imperfect, in part because, as Wittgenstein might say, when we encounter someone whose tongue is impenetrable to us we "cannot find our feet with them." In *Public Man, Private Woman*, I just scratched the surface rather than plumbing the depths of Augustine's bold forays into language and questions of what we now call hermeneutics or interpretation.

Let's take the measure, in however schematic a way, of several of his key themes. First, *contra* much of what has gone under the name Political Augustinianism, a closer look at Augustine on the nature and purpose of social forms and civic life shows us that these are not, crudely, what sin has brought into the world but what man, who is sinful, has wrought through the use of his God-given reason and his capacity for love, as well as his lust for dominance. There is a "darkness that attends the life of human society"[8] and this pertains within, and cuts across, the levels or rings or circles of human existence—the *domus*, or household; the *civitas*, or city, from clans and tribes to great and terrible empires; the *orbis terrae*, or the earth itself; finally, the *mundus*, or universe, the heaven and the earth.

Social life on all levels is full of ills and yet to be cherished. "The philosophers hold the view that the life of the wise man should be social; and in this we support them . . . heartily." The City of God itself could never have made "its first start . . . if the life of the saints were not social."[9] And yet one cannot but sigh and experience with "deep sorrow of heart" the multitude of reports on the ills attendant upon every sphere of social existence. Some are "strong enough to bear these ills with equanimity," but even such a one "cannot but feel grievous anguish, if he himself is a good man, at the wickedness of the traitors." Viciousness and shame may even, horribly, begin at home. "If, then, safety is not to be found in the home, the common refuge from the evils that befall mankind, what shall we say of the city? The larger the city, the more is its forum filled with civil lawsuits and criminal trials, even if that city be at peace, free from alarms or—what is more frequent—the bloodshed of sedition and civil war. It is true that cities are at times exempt from those occurrences; they are never free from the danger of them."[10] What stands in the way of full use of human reason for good? Why are the anguish and the joy of human life so closely intertwined? Augustine provides a veritable hive abuzz with a swarm of explanations, among them his emphasis on the role of language.

In Book XIX, chapter 7, Augustine muses about the way in which all sentient creatures called human are divided by linguistic differences. These differences make it very hard for us to understand one another. Listen to these words:

> [T]he diversity of languages separates man from man. For if two men meet and are forced by some compelling reason not to pass on but to stay in company, then if neither knows the other's language, it is easier for dumb animals, even of different kinds, to associate together than these men, although both are human beings. For when men cannot communicate their thoughts to each other, simply because of difference of language, all the similarity of their common human nature is of no avail to unite them in fellowship. So true is this that a man would be more cheerful with his dog for company than with a foreigner. I shall be told that the Imperial City has been at pains to

impose on conquered peoples not only her yoke but her language also, as a bond of peace and fellowship, so that there should be no lack of interpreters but even a profusion of them. True; but think of the cost of this achievement! Consider the scale of those wars, with all that slaughter of human beings, all the human blood that was shed![11]

This passage surely cheered the somewhat gloomy Wittgenstein! Think of what Augustine here accomplishes. He moves from the murkiness and impenetrability of language, how it divides us *despite* our "common human nature," to the imposition of a language on diverse peoples but at a truly terrible price. We have in this passage a drawing together of notions of human nature, language, and its centrality in constituting us as living creatures; the search for fellowship (sometimes easier to achieve with a dog than a foreigner); and a pithy critique of the enforced homogeneity of empire. My specific concern in recounting this passage in an earlier work was to think through public and private. I suggested that perhaps men and women in past epochs spoke something of a different language even within the boundaries of a single linguistic community, because men had greater access to a public language or rhetoric than women, whose speech was confined to the household. But the heart of Augustine on language lies elsewhere, whatever the truth of my underdeveloped insight. What I am clearer on now is the appeal of what I called "the language of Christianity" to women in the late antique world, because the things Christ held dear and cherished—forgiveness, succor, devotion—helped to forge the terms of their own lives, that and the fact that the Christian rhetoric Augustine at first found inelegant and even vulgar was simple and direct—told in the language of the people, cast in the forms of everyday speech, speech that communicated, speech with a liberatory moment that reached out to incorporate into a new community—the *koinonia*—those who were severed from the classical *polis*, women and the poor.[12] I will have more to say on Augustine on men and women below.

I remain intrigued by the influence of Augustine on Wittgenstein, another topic less fully written about than it might be, perhaps because Wittgenstein has tended to be the purview of analytic philosophers or *verstehen* opponents of analytic philosophers, most of whom do not seem to have taken up Augustine as a companion in thought. Augustine pays meticulous attention to the performative requirements or dimensions of language and acknowledges the importance of convention and conventional understanding. Indeed, in most things we must "follow the conventions in human language" because we cannot leap out of the world and attain an Archimedean point or a meta-language purged of earthly usage by fallible creatures.[13] Augustine knew that no language could be transparent, translucent, perfectly freed from earthly habit, thickening, smudging.

Let me offer up just a few examples. Take the following peroration on the word 'religion':

> the word 'religion' would seem, to be sure, to signify more particularly the 'cult' offered to God, rather than 'cult' in general; and that is why our translators have used it to render the Greek word *thrêskeia*. However, in Latin usage . . . 'religion' is something which is displayed in human relationships, in the family . . . and between friends; and so the use of the word does not avoid ambiguity when the worship of God is in question. We have no right to affirm with confidence that 'religion' is confined to the worship of God, since it seems that this word has been detached from its normal meaning, in which it refers to an attitude of respect in relations between a man and his neighbour.[14]

Augustine performs many such 'Wittgensteinian' operations on central words.

The upshot of the force of linguistic convention is that we human beings have, or can achieve, only our "creature's knowledge" and it comes in "in faded colours, compared with the knowledge that comes when it is known in the Wisdom of God. . . ." Godlike wisdom is not attainable on this earth.[15] Language is mysterious and inexhaustible. It cannot capture the entirety of thought, try as one might, brilliant and learned as one might be. We are both limited *and* enabled by the "accepted conventions of language." For example, these conventions "allow us to 'make use' of 'fruits' and to 'enjoy' the 'use' of things; for 'fruits' are also properly the 'fruits of the earth', and we all 'make use' of them in this temporal life." It is this "common meaning of 'use' I have in mind," Augustine tells us, when I use the word 'use.' The ways in which words divide was not invented by philosophers but, instead, is used by them, sometimes in inventive ways. Yet no philosopher can jump out of his or her linguistic skin.[16]

The upshot is that we "had better conform to normal usage, as indeed we are bound to do, and, for example, to use the phrase 'before death' "—this in a discussion of how we distinguish life from death— "to mean before death occurs, as in the scriptural text: 'Do not praise any man before his death.' "[17] There is much more along these lines, but perhaps these few examples will suffice to alert us to the powerful contours of Augustine's insights as a linguistic philosopher.

Let's consider next his powerful treatment of the inescapability of interpretation from *The Confessions.* Augustine begins by watching babies, as I indicated in chapter 1. This is already a shocking thing for a philosopher to do and to derive epistemological value from. Augustine's is no philosophical anthropology à la Kant, wherein the philosopher devises a set of abstract propositions or presuppositions without concrete attention of any kind to any specific way of life. Augustine notices, remember, that babies throw fits and do all sorts of nasty things, in part because they are trying to make themselves understood and are failing. They get cross because others are not at their "beck and call."[18] By observing babies, he concludes that as they enter the world of speech, they come to appreciate the power of words, including their own.

Through agreed convention one learns an alphabet. But language does more: it both moves one and one is moved by it, by the representations language bears. A speech-user enamored of words and their power can easily get caught up in a spider's web of speech and become "all words," bogged down in conformity to convention in a way that is clichéd and cannot unlock the heart and the mind. A statement is "not necessarily true because it is wrapped in fine language," nor false if it is "awkwardly expressed."[19]

Suppose next that one's heart is unlocked, or is starting to open to God's truth? Can there not be some closure then, some sure and certain way to express the truth of things post-conversion, as it were? Alas, it is not to be. That there is truth is beyond doubt. But there is much that must be figuratively explained, including, or perhaps especially, from Scripture. Augustine tells us of his perplexity with certain passages from the Old Testament. "These passages had been death to me when I took them literally, but once I had heard them explained in their spiritual meaning I began to blame myself for my despair . . . ."[20] Literalist readings may, paradoxically, throw one off the trail of the truth by foreclosing a richness of possible meanings.

The blockbuster Book X of *The Confessions* provides a hermeutical theory that is itself a dense imbrication of multiple meanings. Augustine puts the question: Why should others believe me? How do they know I am telling the truth? And he answers that there are many things one cannot prove; however, those whose ears are opened by charity will be able to listen with their hearts. We are an "inquisitive race," eager to pry, but we often do so from a harshness, a rush to destroy. There is, it seems, a condition of being that makes knowing itself possible, that can stir the heart and thus the mind. Although perfect self-knowledge is never possible, knowledge *is*. There is much we understand because we believe—not, however, from a stance of naive credulity, or because belief somehow brings inquiry to a definitive halt.[21] To the contrary: belief should spur understanding and sustain further inquiry.

The immediate matter before Augustine is memory, that great

storehouse; that depth with its images to which are attached many things in its multiple folds. Epistemically, there is a mystery here, but we can gain a few rather precise intimations. When we hear certain sorts of questions—whether a thing exists, what that thing is, what sort of thing it is—the images cast by the sounds of words trigger recall and knowledge. Attention helps us to collect these scattered images, to draw them together into something recollectable, coherent, that we can offer others. But, of course, I, the curious self, want more than that. I want to understand meaning. (We have now moved to another prodigious accomplishment, Book XI of *The Confessions.*) Truth knows no language—it is "neither Hebrew nor Greek nor Latin nor any foreign speech. . . ."[22] But truth—imperfect truth given voice by human beings—is different from God's speech. God's word is not the speech of discrete words. It is spoken all at once and outside of time. We, however, are caught in time. Only outside of time is the intellect privileged to "know all at once."[23] We are on this earth. We are, therefore, immersed in a world of multiple interpretations—this from Book XII.

Augustine offers an interpretive principle with flexibility. Truth may be singular but meaning is multiple. How can it possibly bring harm "if I understand the writer's meaning in a different sense from that in which another understands it? All of us who read his words do our best to discover and understand what he had in mind, and since we believe that he wrote the truth, we are not so rash to suppose that he wrote anything which we know or think to be false."[24] The text in question is Scripture, so the principle of interpretive charity is particularly exigent. But Augustine adds flesh to the bones of this interpretive charity.

Take, for example, "In the Beginning God made heaven and earth." Augustine offers at least five plausible interpretations, all gesturing toward the truth of that claim. He proliferates examples of this sort and he doesn't stint on making each of the alternatives attractive. There is a classical hermeneutical dilemma we simply cannot get out of. Two sorts of disagreements may arise: (1) concerning the truth of the message and (2) concerning the meaning of the message. We can never plumb fully what was in an author's mind; here there can be no absolute certainty. The realm of immutable truth gives birth to many meanings; the workings of truth are varied epistemologically. "When so many meanings, all of them acceptable as true, can be extracted from the words that Moses wrote, do you not see how foolish it is to make a bold assertion that one in particular is the one he had in mind? Do you not see how foolish it is to enter into mischievous arguments which are an offence against that very charity for the sake of which he wrote every one of the words that we are trying to explain?"[25] In a world of signs, sacraments, miracles, "more things on heaven and earth" than are dreamt of in most philosophies, a truth the mind understands can be materially expressed in a variety of means; thus, "I see nothing to prevent me from interpreting the words of your Scriptures in this figurative sense."[26] I fear this, too, only scratches the surface but we must move on.

The Household and the City: The Good, the Bad, and the Ugly

In the matters of the *domus* and the *civitas*, Augustine once again complexifies our understanding. Rather than bifurcating the earthly sphere into rigidly demarcated public and private realms, Augustine finds in the household "the beginning, or rather a small component part of the city, and every beginning is directed to some end of its own kind, and every component part contributes to the completeness of the whole of which it forms a part. The implication is quite apparent, that domestic peace contributes to the peace of the city—that is, the ordered harmony of those who live together in a house . . . contributes to the ordered harmony concerning authority and obedience obtaining among the citizens."[27] (Although a contemporary feminist would emphasize "gender egalitarianism" rather than "harmony, authority and obedience" and that all-too-human dependence on others that begins in the household, Augustine's insistence on an *internal* relationship between this beginning and what we call civic life is not only compatible with, but a strong buttress of feminist claims that public and private are not hermetically sealed off one from the other.)

Every beginning carries within it a portion of the nature of the whole, even as the whole overlaps with, and is internally connected to, the part. The relation of *domus* to *civitas* is not a grinding of frictional parts, for these spheres of human existence do not diverge as types or in kind; rather, aspects of the whole are borne into the parts, and the integrity and meaning of the part carries forward to become an *integral* part of the whole.[28] Augustine here is engaged in a "*redefinition* of the public itself, designed to show it is life outside the Christian community which fails to be truly public, authentically political. The opposition is not between public and private, church and world, but between political virtue and political vice."[29] Augustine's unpacking of this relationship is fascinating, turning, as it does, on his recognition that the life of the household, the church, and the city is a social life, erected initially—certainly where the household and some form or semblance of society are concerned—on the ground of a naturalistic morality, a basic grammar of human actions and possibilities framed by finitude, by birth and death. Every way of life incorporates injunctions and admonitions and mounts approbrium or generates encomiums in the areas of sexuality, the taking of life, and the grounds of just or fair treatment.

If this feels or seems common-sensical, it probably should, although what is given by nature is not a sufficient basis for civic peace or domestic peace, for that matter. Augustine is convinced that were one to gather together a representative sample of humankind from the far-flung parts of the earth and ask them what they would prefer not to suffer, there would be a surprising (for him not-all-that-surprising) degree of unanimity. No one wants to be tortured or killed. Everyone wants safety and sufficient food and the like. There are rough and ready needs and givens that move people into fellowship with one another. Just as each and every human being and each and every human community is plagued by a "poverty-stricken kind of power . . . a kind of scramble for . . . lost dominions and . . . honours,"[30] so there is simultaneously present the life-forgiving and gentler aspects of loving concern, mutuality, domestic and civic peace.

Because Augustine is so often represented as a dour, late antique Hobbesian, it is worth belaboring this latter insight for a few moments. Here one must introduce two central Augustinian terms that name an earthly struggle that gestures toward ultimate things: *caritas* locked in combat with the contending force of *cupiditas*. This is old hat, so to speak, worn-smooth coin of the realm for Augustinian scholars. But let's see if we can give this a new twist, or, to sustain the metaphor, let's give the coin another toss.

There are two fundamentally different attitudes evinced within human social life and enacted by human beings. One attitude is a powerful feeling of the fullness of life. A human being will not be denuded if he or she gives, or makes a gift of the self, to others. One's dependence on others is not a diminution but an enrichment of self. The other attitude springs from cramped and cribbed pity, from resentment, from a penury of spirit. The way one reaches out or down to others from these different attitudes is strikingly distinct. From a spirit of resentment and contempt, one condescends toward the other; one is hostile to life itself. But from that fellow feeling in our hearts for the misery of others, we come to their help by coming together with them. Authentic compassion (*com*, together; *pati*, to suffer) eradicates contempt and distance. The Christian is not afraid that he or she will lose something by offering him or herself. That is what the ethic of *caritas* is about—not moralistic self-abnegation but an abundant overflowing of the fullness of life.

There is a theology of the household and a theology of the city and they turn on the same things. Augustine deploys analogies in a free-flowing way between the two. The pirate band enjoys a semblance to empire; the robber band's ethics, to justice; even a conspiracy, a kind of peace among associates who are up to no good, exhibits a semblance to peace. For:

> Even in the extreme case when they have separated themselves from others by sedition, they cannot achieve their aim unless they maintain some sort of semblance of peace with their confederates in conspiracy. Moreover, scoundrels and robbers, to ensure greater efficiency and security in their assaults on the peace of the rest of mankind, desire to preserve peace with their associates.[31]

Augustine is second to none, including the inimitable Hobbes, in cataloging the miseries attendant upon human life, the miseries he lays on the doorstep of sin, our division (within selves and between self and others), our enthrallment to *cupiditas* and our all-too-frequent abandonment of *caritas*. We are, in other words, ignorant but it is ignorance of a particular kind, not innocent naivete (if indeed naivete is ever innocent) but prideful cognitive amputation. He writes:

> Such is the clear evidence of that terrifying abyss of ignorance, as it may be called, which is the source of all error, in whose gloomy depths all the sons of Adam are engulfed, so that man cannot be rescued from it without toil, sorrow and fear. What else is the message of all the evils of humanity? The love of futile and harmful satisfactions, with its results: carking anxieties, agitations of mind, disappointments, fears, frenzied joys, quarrels, disputes, wars, treacheries, hatreds, enmities, deceits, flattery, fraud, theft, rapine, perfidy, pride, ambition, envy, murder, parricide, cruelty, savagery, villainy, lust, promiscuity, indecency, unchastity, fornication, adultery, incest, unnatural vice in men and women (disgusting acts too filthy to be named), sacrilege, collusion, false witness, unjust judgement, violence, robbery, and all other such evils which do not immediately come to mind, although they never cease to beset this life of man— all these evils belong to man in his wickedness, and they all spring

from that root of error and perverted affection which every son of Adam brings with him at his birth. For who is not aware of the vast ignorance of the truth (which is abundantly seen in infancy) and the wealth of futile desires (which begins to be obvious in boyhood) which accompanies a man on his entrance into this world, so that if man were left to live as he chose and act as he pleased he would fall into all, or most, of those crimes and sins which I have mentioned—and others which I was not able to mention.[32]

We are no doubt grateful that Augustine stopped his list-making when he did. This passage, taken by itself, would seem to justify the grumpiest readings of the most perfervid political Augustinian. But hold. There is more. There are countervailing influences, as we like to say. A good God's grace and mercy let's take for granted for the sake of Augustine's argument, remaining, therefore, on *terra firma* with him in order to continue to build the case. It is worth returning, at this juncture, to those containers for human social life, those forms and institutions that mark our dependence on one another, our need for trust, our capacity to mark new beginnings and to hope, our embrace—not from desperation but from yearning—of *caritas*. People yearn for earthly peace among friends. Augustine extends the definition of friend. Friends:

> may mean those in the same house, such as a man's wife or children, or any other members of the household; or it can mean all those in the place where a man has his home, a city, for example, and a man's friends are thus his fellow-citizens; or it can extend to the whole world, and include the nations with whom a man is joined by membership of the human society; or even to the whole universe, "heaven and earth" as we term it, and to those whom the philsophers call gods, whom they hold to be a wise man's friends—our more familiar name for them is "angels."[33]

Mind you, friendship can never be carefree, but the "unfeigned faith and mutual affections of genuine, loyal friends" is our indispensable consolation. The "more friends we have and the more dispersed they are in different places, the further and more widely extend our fears that evil may befall them from among all the mass of evils in this present world." Should this happen, "burning sorrow . . . ravages our hearts." But this goes with the territory, so-to-speak. The "consoling delights of friendship" mean the deaths of friends must bring us sadness. "Anyone who forbids such sadness must forbid, if he can, all friendly conversation, must lay a ban on all friendly feeling or put a stop to it, must with a ruthless insensibility break the ties of all human relationships. . . ."[34]

Friendship, then, is the glue that forges our human ties, it binds husband and wife, brother and sister, friend to friend, citizen to citizen, even in the limited and flawed realm of earthly life. For the earthly city is the densely layered site of human designs. And those designs are limited by definition. A principle of interpretive charity might help us to understand and to communicate, despite the fact that each nation possesses its own language. But that household and city are alike containers for charity and cauldrons for ill-will there can be no doubt. Human society in all its aspects is twisted by life within unjust and oppressive earthly dominions and the conceptions under which those dominions order their rule. A Ciceronian definition of a people as a number of persons associated by common acknowledgement of certain rules for right and the pursuit of justice is inadequate, simply not up to the task of recognizing and deepening the work of *caritas*. Rather, as I noted above, we must look to an assemblage of persons bound together by common agreement as to the objects of love.

What are the bases for order and comity in the earthly city? Let's return to the household. Augustine assumes the ontological equality of men and women but accepts that they occupy different offices or stations. There is a basis for this both in convention and in the order of nature. But Augustine hopes to tame the occasions for the reign of *cupiditas*, for the activation of the *libido*

dominandi. It follows that the father in the household should in-
jure none and do good to all. A father who falls down on this job
is worse than an "infidel." It is worth listening to what he says on
this subject in his own words: "those who are genuine 'fathers
of their household' are concerned for the welfare of all in their
households. . . . a man's house ought to be the beginning, or
rather a small component part of the city. . . . The implication is
quite apparent, that domestic peace contributes to the peace of
the city. . . ."[35] The ground of relations of domestic peace is a
well-ordered concord within the family. Both parents share responsibility for their children; women, however, should defer to
their husbands, not because they are unequal to men in the order
of creation, or not fully rational beings (pace Aristotle), but because such deference is provided for in tradition and is necessary
to promote the ends of domestic peace and civic harmony.
(Today, of course, we would argue that deference that flows primarily from wife to husband is not required by Augustine's com-
mitment to ontological equality and may, in fact, exist in tension
with it.)

Augustine warns that the husband's authority must never be
arbitrary and cannot be absolute. He stresses the importance of
households whose foundations lie in compassion and justice,
tempered with mercy. A righteous domestic order is a civitas in
miniature ruled by love, compassion, and authority in the person
of Christian parents. It offers membership in the society of the
faithful during their sojourn on this earth, or one form of membership, at any rate. The Church is another body of friends. The
city yet another. But the temptations of arbitrary power and excess grow greater the more power there is to be had. The life of
virtue is a shared life, but so is the life of perfidy. Absolute mastery, or the urgency to acquire it, severs human beings from one
another, often violently. For he who would be master—whether a
brutal paterfamilias, a ruthless leader of a robber band, or an avari-
cious emperor—needs other human beings to work on and to
work over, quite literally.

If *cupiditas* gains the upper hand, the result is deepening misery. Any argument that asserts that this dominion, these forms of violent or coercive imposition, is natural is wrong. For we are not, as I have already noted, political by nature. Politics results from concatenated acts of human willing, human design. Thus, Augustine can be drawn upon not only to defeat the claims of *imperium*, or to chasten these claims, but to tame the rule by fathers as well. For here things are somewhat reversed. The father's natural responsibility for, and authority within, the *domus* is not a political right and does not translate into one. Political authority in the *civitas* is similar to, yet different from, that of the ruler to subject. Augustine protested assimilating paternal and political authority even as he drew analogies between them.

Small wonder so few get him right. This is complicated stuff. The calling of nature may move us into fellowship with one another. But nature's reign is not sufficient unto itself. Human projects, for better or worse, must be enacted. And they must be chastened, tempered with the life-sustaining honey of *caritas*. The fullness of this honeyed life remains for the heavenly city— Augustine, in a letter, speaks of being enrolled "as a citizen of a country which is above, in holy love, for which we endure perils and toils . . . ." Earthly cities too often inflame us, they are ablaze with arms. The flowers are threaded through with thorns. To a citizen of such an earthly city, in this same letter, Augustine writes:

> Look for a moment at those very books "On the State" from which you imbibed that sentiment of a loyal subject, that "to good men there is no limit or end of devotion to their country." [Sound familiar?] Look at them, I pray you, and notice the praise with which frugality and self-control are extolled, and fidelity to the marriage-bond, and chaste, honourable, and upright character. When a country is distinguished for these qualities, it may truly be said to be in full flower.[36]

Then and then alone. But one must remain vigilant.

There are, for example, among the pagans, more or less virtuous objects of emulation and admiration. Unfortunately, as John Milbank observes, "The Romans, like all pagans, think there can be virtue where there is something to be defeated, and virtue therefore consists for them, not only in the attainment and pursuit of a goal desirable in itself, but also in a 'conquest' of less desirable forces, which is always an exercise of strength *supplementary to*, although supporting, a 'right desire.' "[37]

The sin that marks the *civitas terrena* is the story of arbitrary power, or the ever-present possibility of such, untempered, as the story of this sin is, with an alternative beginning point—the privileging of peace over war; indeed the ontological priority of peace.[38] Pilgrims on this earth understand that life around them was created by human beings to achieve some good, to avoid greater evil. Augustine's work is not about flight from the world. His recurrent theme, as Peter Brown reminds us, is "our business within this common mortal life."[39] My discussion of that peace which is "dear to the hearts" of humankind awaits chapter 5 below. More will also be provided on the earthly city at that time. But, finally, let me turn to a controversial arena, the story of men and women in Augustine.

Male and Female, Created He Them

Augustine's principle of charitable interpretation is in place as I begin, not because I want to let Augustine off the hook but because I want to rescue him from reckless charges of misogyny, a much overused word that has become debased coin of our discursive realm. (It is worth remembering that misogyny was— for those who originated the term—a terrible disorder, the actual *hatred* of women. It was not garden variety male dominance of which the world has no doubt had quite enough. But misogyny was named by the ancients as a derangement; thus, the misogynist was not upheld as a right-thinking sort of guy, a regular fellow.) Let's begin with Augustine's wonderfully generous definition of humanity. Men and women share a nature. The woman's mind and rational intelligence are "the equal of man's."⁴⁰ As well, the entire sentient human race belongs within one category, the human, for God created us all, male and female, diverse races, even bizarre creatures most of us would scarcely call human, though Augustine did. Celebrating God's diversity within the unity of creation, Augustine embarks on a description that delights, a discourse of "recorded monstrosities." He begins by telling us that there are many accounts—his own chief authority is Pliny's *Natural History*—of strange creatures whose existence raises some questions about human derivation and definition. There are:

> the [so-called] *Sciopods* ('shadow-feet') because in hot weather they lie on their backs on the ground and take shelter in the shade of their feet. . . . What am I to say of the *Cynocephali*, whose dog's head and actual barking prove them to be animals rather than men? Now we are not bound to believe in the existence of all the types of men which are described. But no faithful Christian should doubt that anyone who is born anywhere as a man—that is, a rational and mortal being—derives from that one first-created human being. And this is true, however extraordinary such a creature may appear to our senses in bodily shape, in colour, or motion, or utterance, or in any natural endowment, or part, or quality. However, it is clear what constitutes the persistent norm of nature in the majority and what, by its very rarity, constitutes a marvel. . . . For God is the creator of all, and he himself knows where and when any creature should be created or should have been created. He has the wisdom to weave the beauty of the whole design out of the constituent parts, in their likeness and diversity. . . . If these races are included in the definition of the 'human', that is, if they are rational and mortal animals, it must be admitted that they trace their lineage from that same one man, the first father of all mankind.⁴¹

To celebrate unity within the diversity of sentient humanity, and diversity within the unity, is a central feature of Augustine's work. Although Augustine doesn't focus on women as a separate consideration in his discussion of the earthly civitas, his enormously expanded definition of what it means to belong to the category human, and his insistence on a basic grammar of morality written on the human heart, touches women directly. Augustine is one of the great undoers of antique philosophies which dictated a separate and inferior female nature and consigned women to a lesser realm dictated by necessity. Because, for Augustine, all human life is lived on the razor's edge of necessity, and because beginnings and human regeneration are his central metaphors, women move much nearer center stage in his scheme of things. As well, the notion of moral revolt against public power opened up a range of options, duties, responsibilities, dilemmas, and reassessments not possible in pre-Christian epochs—for males and females alike.

What Augustine struggled with in the matter of men and women helps to illuminate many current debates and concerns. Adam and Eve, for example, are both responsible for the entry of sin into the world. Augustine's story of the Fall is a story of the "first human beings." His reference point is "they"—they "did not deny their sin . . . their pride seeks to pin the wrong act on another; the woman's pride blames the serpent, the man's pride blames the woman."[42] Both allowed themselves to be tempted. Both committed offenses. Both tried to pass the buck. In De Trinitate he insists that the woman along with the man "completes the image of the Trinity," for "human nature itself, which is complete in both sexes, has been made to the image of God, and he does not exclude the woman from being understood as the image of God."[43] He goes on to ask: "Who is it, then, that would exclude women from this fellowship, since they are co-heirs of grace," reminding his readers that through baptism male and female alike "have put on Christ." Therefore, "in their minds, a common nature is recognized, but in their bodies the division of this one mind itself is symbolized."[44]

He returns to the creation story yet another time and argues that the woman did not eat the forbidden fruit alone; therefore, it is outrageous to argue that "the woman, as it were, can be condemned without the man. Far be it from us to believe this!"[45] Performative requirements flow from this ontology of equality. "Let the husband render unto the wife due benevolence; and likewise also the wife unto the husband. The wife hath not power of her own body, but the husband; and likewise also the husband hath not power of his own body, but the wife."[46] Some might suggest, a bit cynically: "Big deal! How does this cash out?" Here it is worth quoting at some length a letter from Augustine to "Brother Eusebius." One point of the letter is to insist that no one be driven "into the Catholic communion against his will. . . ." But he has other fish to fry, an "abominable" matter concerning a "young man" who is "rebuked by his bishop for repeatedly thrashing his mother like a madman and for not withholding his unfilial hands from the body that gave him birth. . . . He threatens his mother to go over to the Donatist party and to do her to death, used as he is to thrash her with unbelievable ferocity." This "raging for his mother's blood," this gross plan of "matricide" must not be tolerated. That the young man in question is still at the altar-rails of the Catholic Church is an insult to the congregation, given his habituation to violence. Augustine tells Eusebius this cannot go on. The Church "forbids my beating my mother." Augustine then analogizes from beating "the body which bore and nurtured" this "thankless son," to the young man's beating of his other mother, that is, to abuse of *mater ecclesia*.[47] This is a fascinating discussion and only too up-to-date, but it does give us some insight into the forms of behavior the Church was attempting to halt. The story of the interdiction of infanticide by the Church is well-known, as is the fact that girl babies were more often exposed than boy babies. But the alteration in human sociality extended beyond that, as Augustine's letter indicates.

There is more. He repudiates propitiation to Fortune, represented as an unpredictable, arbitrary, erratic, and feminized cosmic force. He attacks Priapus ("that all too male god"), whose rites involved the public humiliation of virgins. He defends the violated virtues of women raped in war, insisting that women should not punish themselves, although inevitably such an event engenders a sense of shame. But violation without the will's consent cannot pollute the character. He writes: "We have given clear reason for our assertion that when physical violation has involved no change in the intention of chastity by any consent to the wrong, then the guilt attaches only to the ravishers, and not at all to the woman forcibly ravished without any consent on her part.... Will our opponents dare to contradict us?"[48] He goes on to tell us that in his pastoral tasks he administered consolation to women who "felt the pangs of shame," urging them "not to be ashamed at being alive, since they have no possible reason for being ashamed at having sinned."[49] Here Augustine challenges the constant attention to reputation required of noble Roman women, a demand that called upon women who had been violated to defend their honor by committing suicide. He also attacks the Lex Vaconia, which forbade the appointment of a woman, even an only daughter, as heir: "I cannot cite, or even imagine, a more inequitable law."[50]

Perhaps most importantly, whatever his acquiescence in the received social arrangements of his time, Augustine left as a permanent legacy a condemnation of that lust for dominion which distorts the personality, marriage, the family, and all other aspects of political and social life. "He who desires the glory of possession," Augustine notes, "would feel that his power were diminished if he were obliged to share it with any living associate," for he is one who cherishes his own manhood.[51]

Finally, there are the metaphors. God's requirement of obedience is "in a way the mother and guardian of all other virtues," not the father.[52] God's grace is given voice in Scripture through women; for example, Hannah, Samuel's mother. Augustine taxes the blindly self-righteous man who despises himself and Christ "on account of the body which he received from a woman...."[53] He says to his imagined interlocutor, "Perhaps you were put off by the unexampled birth of his body from a virgin? But this should not have presented a difficulty. The fact that a wonderful being was born in a wonderful way ought rather to induce you to accept our religion."[54] Lest anyone suspect that it is only virgin births that are wonderful to Augustine, consider his repeated use of the metaphor of laboring and giving birth to describe his own activities in trying to bring forth a transformed way of understanding his own self.[55] No man who loathed all things female could possibly characterize himself in this fleshly and feminized way. Even that city for which the *peregrinus* yearns is a mother, Jerusalem our Mother.

> By 'Jerusalem', moreover, we must understand not the Jerusalem which is enslaved along with her children, but our free mother, the Jerusalem which, according to the Apostle, is eternal in the heavens. There, after the hardships of our anxieties and worries in this mortal state we shall be comforted like little children carried on the mother's shoulders and nursed in her lap. For that unaccustomed bliss will lift us up, untrained and immature as we are, and support us with tenderest caresses.[56]

We may "rocka our souls in the bosom of Abraham," but we are held in the lap of our Mother.

3

Against the Pridefulness of
Philosophy

We don't like limits very much. The 'we' I have in mind is late modern human beings in general and Americans in particular. Americans, especially, live in an unusually free and driven culture. Being an American means, or meant, being new, a different sort of creature unsullied by the old, the worn-out, the corrupted. We want to succeed at our jobs or careers. We want to succeed as students. We want to succeed as lovers and mates. We want to succeed as parents. We want to be successful at success.

Most of the time we don't think about a philosophy behind all of this. Why bother? We can get along quite well without it, thank you. Yet there is a philosophy at work, at least in the story of success as untrammeled individual striving. This philosophy can be named a variety of ways. Augustine's name for it would be the "sin of pride." This, I know, goes over like a lead balloon. We don't believe in sin anymore—we believe in syndromes—and pride is what we need and want and we want it now. We are told that our lives will be as ashes and ruins in our mouths if we don't have a sufficient SEQ: self-esteem quotient.

Augustine certainly doesn't want people to run around being abject. In fact, he frets frequently about the ways in which self-abnegation can turn into forms of boasting and unseemly display. In a letter, he writes—the year is 423 A.D.—"pride lurks even in good deeds to their undoing." One can take excessive pride in humbling oneself and this, in turn, has a corrupting effect not only on oneself but on the recipient of one's display of largesse, leading to such abominable travesties "of monastic life whereby the rich, as far as possible, are to be compelled to toil, and the poor allowed to live in luxury."[1] This reversal in domination defeats *caritas*, hence the possibility for authentic brotherhood, representing, instead, a victory for *cupiditas*. Augustine worried about *ressentiment* long before Nietzsche, arguing that Christ calls us to strength, not to weakness, and certainly not to exhibitions of our own humility. To repeat: pride "lurks even in good deeds to their undoing."[2]

False pride, pride that turns on the presumption that we are the sole and only ground of our own being; denying our birth from the body of a woman; denying our utter dependence on her and others to nurture and tend to us; denying our continuing dependence on friends and family to sustain us; denying our dependence on our Maker to guide and to shape our destinies, here and in that life in the City of God for which Augustine so ardently yearned, is, then, the name Augustine gives to a particular form of corruption and human deformation. Pridefulness denies our multiple and manifold dependencies and would have us believe that human beings can be masters of their fates, or Masters of the Universe as currently popular super-heroes are named. Those who refuse to recognize dependence are those most overtaken by the urgency of domination, or "the need to secure the dependence of others," an observation from Peter Brown, who goes on to argue that "first the Devil, then Adam, chose to live on their own resources; they preferred their own *fortitudo*, their own created strength, to dependence upon the strength of God. For this reason, the deranged relationships between fallen angels and men show themselves in a constant effort to assert their incomplete power by subjecting others to their will."[3] Every "proud man heeds himself, and he who pleases himself seems great to himself. But he who pleases himself pleases a fool, for he himself is a fool when he is pleasing to himself," Augustine writes.[4]

I will have more to say about limits in chapter 5. My primary target in this chapter is the pridefulness of philosophy. What do I mean by this? I mean the presumption that one can master knowledge and attain epistemic completeness and certainty through one's own, unaided efforts. I mean the will to power manifested in the creation of huge systems of thought that try to seal every crack, close off every air vent, plug every hole. I mean the arrogant certainty evinced by some philosphers who believe a day is wasted unless they have wasted someone else in a knock-down argument of one sort or another. (One might call this the destruction of dialogue.) I mean *reductios* of all kind that hive off one bit of human motivation and make that the whole. I mean a refusal to recognize finitude itself, hence our own radical incompleteness. Perhaps this latter recognition helps to account for Augustine's refusal to systematize and his story-telling, allegorical style.[5] Clearly, I mean lots of things, so let's get started.

Knowledge of Mind

Can the mind ever really know itself? On the one hand, we have learned to have great doubts about this, doubts fueled in part by Freud's revolution—I meant the great Sigmund, not many of the lesser epigones—but doubts long voiced in the Western tradition. Part of this doubt is a coming to grips with the pervasiveness of mental conflict and the phenomenon that was called *backsliding* when I was growing up—our inability to hold consistently to a stance of moral achievement, least of all perfection. When current critics talk about a triumphalistic, logocentric metanarrative and indict the Western tradition or Euro-centrism, I, as I have already indicated, am unsure they know what they are talking about when the claim is that sweeping. Augustine, in fact, would be an ally in critiques of Hegelian overcoming (and what Marx and, even worse, such avatars of ethically bereft mastery as J. P. Sartre did with Hegelianism); would help to challenge the magical work of a dialectic that can turn dross, including repugnant and remorseless violence, into historic gold. Augustine was no proto-Kantian either, in this sense. He recognized that in a world of finitude there are tragic things that happen and morally murky decisions to be made. Goods can conflict: hence, the tragedy of necessary wars. Yet Augustine remains an irritant to us bold postmoderns who believe we are daring to go where no human being has gone before. He was there before us. Let's turn, therefore, to Augustine's powerful mind as it [he] grappled with mind itself.

Augustine is sometimes seen as a being in a headlong plunge from reason into that heart of darkness the enlightened think of as faith. Wrong. He is in flight from a distorted love of reason. My primary text will be *De Trinitate*, The Trinity, one of the great works in the philosophy of mind, although, of course, it is much more than that. Or, perhaps better put, given the generosity and complexity of what Augustine packs into mind, the book moves back and forth from mind's knowledge of itself, to self and mind, to self and others, to self and God, and so on. The best I can do is to call up a few passages and arguments in order to try to elaborate on them as fairly and succinctly as possible.

We begin at the beginning, with an infant. We do not start out in a pristine state of mind and being.[6] We are driven by hunger, need, and, early on, jealousy, as well as sheer frustration at our inability to express ourselves transparently and to get others to respond instantly. Growing up is not about getting rid of these childish emotions—these are key ingredients of our natures and our ability to understand—hence Augustine's withering fire directed at Stoic *apatheia*. For the mind to be in a "state in which the mind cannot be touched by any emotion whatsoever, who would not judge this insensitivity to be the worst of all moral defects?"[7] This latter stance invites the "stupefying arrogance" of those "who imagine that they find the Ultimate Good in this life and that they can attain happiness by their own efforts. . . . What a life of bliss, that seeks the aid of death to end it! If this is happiness, let him continue in it!"[8]

No, we are beings who love, who yearn, and who experience frustration, pretty much from the start. Our words and meanings and signs and gestures are always open to misunderstanding; always subject to multiple, ambiguous interpretation. The child gets "launched . . . into the stormy life of human society," and it is no smooth launching.[9] But it's awfully interesting. There may be "a very great difference between a boy and a mature man, yet no one, if asked each day from boyhood on, will at any given time declare that he has reached maturity."[10] Except, perhaps, Augustine might coyly add, the one who calls himself a philosopher. Too often, he has lost sight of the role love and desire play in perceiving and knowing—persistently, not as a first stab at knowing, or as a preliminary skirmish. Such a one does not know what it is like to wander "in the sweet meadows of Christ."[11] Even in evoking his Lord, Augustine cannot but be lyrical and extol the delights of the world.

What captures our interest? Our selves, for one thing. Because we are driven by *delectio*, by desire and yearning, we search for enjoyment, including pleasures of the intellect. The intellect must be *engaged*, Augustine argues, before it can rise.[12] "And as a general rule, there is no other way in which the human spirit can acquire self-knowledge except by trying its own strength in answering, not in word but in deed, what may be called the interrogation of temptation."[13] These inquiries are necessarily flawed. But they fascinate us if we are living, breathing, engaged creatures. And we are drawn to our own minds because they are a ground of our existence.

I am certain I exist, in part because I can be mistaken; in part because I doubt. "Then since my being mistaken proves that I exist, how can I be mistaken in thinking that I exist, seeing that my mistake establishes my existence?"[14] Might we say: I doubt and I make mistakes, therefore I am? This is pretty much what Augustine suggests and it isn't the sort of clarion call to self-certain arms most philosophers would endorse. The truth is characterized by its hiddenness and "ignorance is unavoidable—and yet the exigences of human society make judgement also unavoidable."[15] Great secrets—of Scripture, of mind, of self, of the world—are, as Augustine says over and over again, "locked away."

How can mind even begin to unlock things? Charles Norris Cochrane, in his enduring classic *Christianity and Classical Culture*, explores Augustine's understanding of mind and consciousness and speaks of what, on Augustine's view, we simply must accept as the fundamental elements of consciousness, including form and matter as "spectacles" through which we see the world.[16] As beings circumscribed by bounds of time and space, we require certain fundamental categories in order to *see* the world at all. Form, which circumscribes, is also a presupposition of freedom, necessary to our very ability to reason things through and to imagine.[17] The primary form, for Augustine, is that form and form-giving category we call the Trinity, "a principle capable of saving the reason as well as the will, and thus redeeming human personality as a whole."[18] Immersed in the flux of time and space, with no possibility of escape, authentic knowledge chastens rather than inflates us. Working dialogically and analogically, working with and through hypostases, essences, similarities, and dissimilarities, Augustine maps Trinity to mind; mind to Trinity. Augustine's much-heralded neoplatonism here gives way, in part. He upends the Platonic dialectic by forsaking the notion that human beings might ever obtain clairvoyant knowledge of transcendent forms. We can, at best, approximate, analogize, allegorize.

By at least partially dethroning knowledge in favor of love, Augustine alerts us to what antique philosophers seemed to "have little appreciation for," according to James Wetzel, namely, "the difficulties creatures of habits and passion . . . have in appropriating philosophical wisdom."[19] The philosophers abstract from, or offer unreal assessments of, our human condition by taking insufficient account of embodiment. The body is epistemically significant, a source of delight, of travail, of knowledge of good and evil. The body is the mode through which we connect to the world and through which the world discloses itself. We, too, are creatures, known to ourselves in part through our relation to other creatures. Creatures cannot aspire to omniscience.[20] "For in this world fear, grief, toil and peril, are unavoidable, but it is of the utmost importance for what cause, with what hope, and to what end a man endures those things."[21]

Mind is embodied; body is thought. The rational soul is engaged through sense perceptions, desire, and then the need to assess, to affirm or to refuse to affirm, in other words, to judge. The heart of Augustine's case against the Pelagians lies here, in their absolutizing of human will, of *voluntas*. Willing is not synonymous with the *choice* of our current dominant discourse. It is more complex by far. To *will* is simultaneously to *nill*, or to entertain the possibility of nilling. Wetzel throws down the gauntlet: "I submit that the Pelagian will is a fiction. There is no faculty of will, distinct from desire, which we use to determine our actions." For: "Pelagius seemed in the end to deny that there were ever significant obstacles to living the good life, once reason had illuminated its nature, [thus] he stood in more obvious continuity with the philosophical tradition than Augustine, who came to disparage the worldly wisdom of pagan philosophy for its overconfidence."[22] Augustine is clear on this score: we cannot sustain a sinless condition; we cannot, *pace* Pelagius, by our own unaided efforts, even with the grace of God, "live without sin, and the fact of having sinned does not prevent a man from turning from it at a future date."[23] The sinless life is a chimera and a dangerous one at that. The complex and tensioned-filled aspects of human experience are effaced if we reify choice and exalt the chooser.

Let us, then, return to Trinity, a pattern that is somewhat accessible in part because it can be represented and experienced immanently, so to speak. It is food for thought. Augustine works from a stance of epistemic *urgency* by contrast to epistemic triumphalism. Augustine is inflamed; he would "joyfully . . . give my pen a holiday," but there is too much to be offered; the principle of charity requires nothing less than to make one's best ef-

fort.[24] We require many who differ in style to write "many
books, even on the same topics, in order that the subject itself
may reach as many people as possible, to some in one way, to
others in a different way," a recognition of the importance of
genre and rhetorical style and occasions, even when approaching
the gravamen of Trinity.[25] We begin with love, urgency, and bodies. Touch—the tactile, the palpable, as well as to be reached, to
be touched—"sets as it were a limit to knowledge."[26] The form
in and through which knowledge can be made manifest to us requires that we first "empty" ourselves in order that we might
"receive" that which is available.[27] The metaphors are fascinating
and fascinatingly feminine, if I may dare say so, having to do
with collecting, emptying, receiving, rather than mastering, at-
tacking, gaining.

Our language and contexts offer us "probable arguments" for
that form we call Trinity. There is, first, provision in language;
there are "significant clues" all over the place; our grasp is uncertain but grasp we must. Although "no language suffices" and
God is utterly Other (as we might now say), He is apprehendable
through a Mediator. God has "come down" to us so we might
"ascend" to Him. All this is at once difficult yet possible because
"the usage of our language has already decided that the same
thing is to be understood when we say essence, as when we say
substance, we do not venture to use the formula one essence and
three substances, but rather one essence or substance and three
persons."[28] Language itself, then, *decides* certain things. Because,
as I have already argued, we cannot leap out of our linguistic
skins, we must work with the repertoire of possibilities language
makes available. We have words like *gift* and *giver* and *mutual* and
communion and *pledge*. We know there are things that can "mutu-
ally correspond to each other" without losing distinctiveness.[29]

We know enough, in other words, to come to know that
which is called Trinity. That form, in turn, affords other occasions for thought. Although our human "speech is confined," it

is not utterly powerless to convey something of "the ineffable."[30] What we cannot grasp "by our reason, let it be held fast by our faith," an injunction unlikely to move most of our contemporaries.[31] This is the famous *credo ut intelligam* derided by Freud (among others) as an invitation to superstition and credulity. But Augustine was no irrationalist. For him, faith and reason were correlative and complementary aspects of experience, a point made by Cochrane and, more recently, by Pope John Paul II in his "Apostolic Letter on Augustine of Hippo," when he writes that Augustine steered between "reason and faith" as the "two forces that . . . cooperate to bring the human person to know the truth. . . ."[32] Thus, Augustine navigated the rough waters between the extremes of a fideism that despises reason and a rationalism that excludes faith. He granted wide epistemic berth to what we would now call natural science.[33] Whatever can be explained in this way, let it be so. The mistake lies in thinking that *everything* can fall under a single epistemic domain. Although it is impossible, within an Augustinian frame, to separate mind and self, because language makes provision for this distinction, I am taking advantage of it to move to knowledge of the self.

Knowledge of Self

The self is a self that is tempted, that yearns, and that imagines. If we would avoid being "hurled into the abyss of our own theories," we must take account of this creature.[34] This is not always a pleasant thing. Self-knowledge brings sorrow but it also brings delight, including "visions suitable to our exile. . . ."[35] There is light shining in that darkness! We are much assisted in our epistemic searches by the Creator who offered the world for delight and contrast. Struck by its beauty, we engage it. Thus "the beauty of the day was enhanced by comparison with the night"; through contrasts, we come to know.[36] The self that recognizes beauty, and is filled with wonder, is a source of value and knowl-

edge, but not *absolute* value and not *perfect* knowledge. Take, for
example, the perils and possibilities of imagining. We form con-
cepts about things we have seen and things we have not seen. We
imagine many things to be, in part because we know what it
means to have, or to bear, the "trace" of an image. We believe
many things exist that are not personally known to us.

> And in fact when I wish to speak of Carthage, I seek for what to say
> within myself, and find an image of Carthage within myself; but I
> received this through the body, that is, through the sense of the
> body, since I was present there in the body, and have seen and per-
> ceived it with my senses, and have retained it in my memory, that I
> might find the word about it within myself whenever I might wish
> to utter it. For its image in my mind is its word, not the sound of
> three syllables when Carthage (*Carthago*) is named, or even when
> that name itself is silently thought of during some period of time,
> but the word that I see in my mind when I utter this word of three
> syllables with my voice, or even before I utter it. . . . So too, when I
> wish to speak of Alexandria which I have never seen, an image of it
> is also present within me.[37]

Augustine uses the metaphor of fabrication—of making
things—in order to try to drive home this point. "A worker
makes a chest. At first he has the chest in his skill-knowledge: For
if he did not have it in his skill-knowledge, how could it be
brought forth by making? But the chest as it is in his skill-
knowledge is not the chest as it appears to our eyes. In skill-
knowledge it exists invisibly, in the work it will exist visibly."[38]
When we gaze upon things in the mind, through a complex
word-name-image nexus (and the analogy to the Trinity is being
worked up by Augustine here as a reasonable thing), we are not
altogether untrammeled in this imagining. There is, so to speak,
an available repertoire. It is linguistic, as I have already observed.
It is historic and thus contingent. It is time-bound. It is caught
within the confines of the limits of our embodiment. So, although naming and imagining is "wonderful," it is also con-

strained. We cannot imagine just anything. If, as Wittgenstein says, a lion could speak we could not understand him, so we can say that if a giraffe could imagine, we could not recognize the imagining. We are not nibbling off treetops and gazing across the savannah from a great height! (That and more, of course, but I assume the reader takes the point.)

Now we come to *see* Trinity through imagining, through naming, and through love. And this love provides the horizon for our account of selfhood. In loving God, we also love our neighbor. If we, in Václav Havel's words, "forget that we are not God," it is easier to forget our neighbor as we begin to tiptoe through the tulips of the Selfsame, when the mind becomes based on itself. Words are not *mere*—they signify and they help to constitute a wonderful human capacity. We love our own faculty to perceive the truth and we love the "splendor of the truth."[39] We yearn for the truth and labor to know it. Through this process the "beauty of minds that have been brought together in fellowship by listening to and answering questions through signs that are known," is made possible and secured.[40] Here Augustine builds a powerful argument against philosophical solipcism, as well as an argument against constituting the self as its own ground.

> How the mind may seek and find itself is, therefore, a remarkable question: whither does it go in order to seek, and whither does it come in order to find? For what is so much in the mind as the mind? . . . As the mind, therefore, is within, it goes in some way outside of itself when it directs the affection of its love towards these sensible things which leave their footprints, as it were, in our mind because we have thought of them so often. These footprints are, so to speak, impressed on the memory when the corporeal things which are without are so perceived that, even when they are absent, their images are present to those who think of them.[41]

I know that I have memory, understanding, and will. I understand that I understand. I will that I will. I remember that I remember, and so on.[42] The mind's power in relation to the body is great. The

mind can alter the "quality" of the "carnal garment," as, for example, when we are "beguiled in sleep" by powerful images.[43]
The body enables but also limits. Thinking is limited by memory.
Augustine compares the limit to perception that lies in the body,
with the limit to thinking that lies in the memory.[44] We must
bring both mind and body to bear, so to speak, if we are really to
comprehend. Augustine calls this "attention," reminding us of a
commonplace experience, that of reading a page or a letter and,
having finished, not knowing what one has read and having to do
it over again; or walking somewhere and 'coming to' and not
knowing how one got there. Just as the weakness of the mind
cannot grasp certain things in a translucent or pellucid form, so
the weakness of the body limits what we can do to, with, or for it.
Yet we *are*; we, our-selves, are a basic datum of experience.

> On the other hand who would doubt that he lives, remembers, un-
> derstands, wills, thinks, knows, and judges? For even if he doubts,
> he lives; if he doubts, he remembers why he doubts; if he doubts, he
> understands that he doubts; if he doubts, he wishes to be certain; if
> he doubts, he thinks; if he doubts, he knows that he does not know;
> if he doubts, he judges that he ought not to consent rashly.[45]

Knowledge of the World

The world beckons and it enchains. This is not an "either . . .
or," it is a "both . . . and." It is almost as if even trees and plants
were reaching out to us, seeking to be known. There is "something like sensitivity in their powers of taking nutriment and of
reproduction. Yet these and all other material things have their
causes hidden in nature; but they offer their forms to the perception of our senses, those forms which give loveliness to the
structure of this visible world. It almost seems as if they long to
be known, just because they cannot know themselves."[46] We
creatures called human "apprehend them by our bodily sense,"
but we go beyond these senses—of "eye, ear, smell, taste or

touch" to an idea and a name in order to get to know that which beckons to us, and through this dynamic process, "I love both existence and knowledge, and am sure that I love them."[47] Augustine even speculates on what the being of a tree must be. "If we were trees, we should not indeed be able to love anything with any sensual emotion; yet we would seem to have a kind of desire for increased fertility and more abundant fruitfulness." Even "stones, waves, wind or flame" that lack sense and life still exhibit "something like a desire" for their own place and order.[48]

Notice how different this version of knowledge of the world is from knowledge that is a form of mastery and appropriation, where what I come to know I must make my own, exploit, and dominate with no reference to the integrity of the thing's own being. Augustine's trees are *longing* somehow to be known, as if they ache from the absence of their own powers of apprehension. Flowers lift up their faces to us. Why are they so beautiful if not to capture our attention and bring us to them, to know them somehow? The world is an overflowing abundance, a consolation to *all* humankind, not a singular benefit or reward "of the blessed." Augustine is worth citing at some length here in order to show the descriptive delectation he offers, evidence of what Peter Brown calls Augustine's immoderate love of the world.

> The manifold diversity of beauty in sky and earth and sea; the abundance of light, and its miraculous loveliness, in sun and moon and stars; the dark shades of woods, the colour and fragrance of flowers; the multitudinous varieties of birds, with their songs and their bright plumage; the countless different species of living creatures of all shapes and sizes, amongst whom it is the smallest in bulk that moves our greatest wonder—for we are more astonished at the activities of tiny ants and bees than at the immense bulk of whales. Then there is the mightly spectacle of the sea itself, putting on its changing colours like different garments, now green, with all the many varied shades, now purple, now blue. Moreover, what a delightful sight it is when stormy, giving added pleasure to the specta-

tor because of the agreeable thought that he is not a sailor tossed and heaved about on it. Think too of the abundant supply of food everywhere to satisfy our hunger, the variety of flavours to suit our pampered taste, lavishly distributed by the riches of nature, not produced by the skill and labour of cooks! Think, too, of all the resources for the preservation of health, or for its restoration, the welcome alternation of day and night, the soothing coolness of the breezes, all the material for clothing provided by plants and animals. Who could give a complete list of all these natural blessings?"[49]

Who indeed? And yet there are troubles aplenty in our engagement with this world. Pain, for example, plain old-fashioned physical pain, is one sign of life. To suffer, one must be alive.[50] But perhaps more importantly, what we create over time in our engagement with the world and that self which engages the world, may get rigidified; we may become focused on ourselves and habituated to self-exaltation: "to exist in oneself, that is to please oneself, is not immediately to lose all being; but it is to come nearer to nothingness. That is why the proud are given another name in holy Scripture; they are called 'self-pleasers.'"[51] When we set our sights too high we wind up diminished. We start to regard ourselves in our own light and we turn into dim bulbs.

As a chain of servitude is encased, encrusted, and becomes second nature, we bind ourselves to ourselves through bad willing, leading, in turn, to actions flowing from the *libido dominandi* that, over time, become habitual. Finally, we no longer recognize the willing involved, for the habit has become a necessity. This story is most fully told in *The Confessions*, of course, but it is a map of the self's engagement with the world Augustine presents repeatedly. Suppose we are caught in a chain of servitude. How do we break up this construction? Change must come from alteration in willing at that juncture because habituation, precisely because it is habituation, cannot begin anything new.[52] It is important to note here, however, that alteration in willing does not mean from the ground of one's own separated being. One can be jogged by one's engagement with the world and others into a reengagement of the will. But if one has, in a sense, *become* one's habits, then to proclaim loudly change "from the self," is all too often to delude. Even if we try, we cannot carry out our own commands because the will does not fully order itself; we are at odds with ourselves.

Why? For one thing, the thickness and density of memory blocks transparent self-knowledge, for in its vast storehouse of images, there are some representations that can be recalled immediately, but many cannot. There are things we sense that are "secreted in folds of the memory storehouse."[53] Astonishingly and disconcertingly, the memory can picture colors in darkness and, in silence, hold sounds. We can never entirely plumb its depths. Memory invites really complex epistemic queries. For example, when I hear certain sorts of questions I must ask *whether* a thing is, *what* it is, and *what sort* it is. I must collect things together through attention.[54] Famously, Augustine has become a problem to himself. He asks: What, then, is my nature? It is "ever varying, full of change, and of immense powers."[55] This is the being that engages the world. This is the being the world engages. This is the being that searches for happiness. This is the being that speculates on dreams "where images of former habits that during the day are deprived of their power" appear with full force when one sleeps, and yet I *am* myself when I sleep. Here there are emanations of Plato, of course, but also presagings of Freud.

Small wonder that a being this varying and this complex must be roused and shaken up from time to time if he or she is to pay real attention once again. Augustine sees Scripture playing this role—not alone, of course, but importantly. Scripture takes us by the scruff of the neck and gives us a good shaking— "to terrify the proud, to arouse the careless, to exercise the inquirer, and to nourish the intelligent; and it would not have this effect if it did not first bend down and, as we may say, descend to the level of those on the ground."[56] Only God enjoys what we call "peace of mind," despite the advertisements on our television sets telling us that we can buy it—peace of mind—as well as all the delectation and distraction we desire.

One night—and it could be *any* night in America now—as I was channel surfing, I stumbled upon a cable channel that runs a regularly scheduled program on "Real Things" or "True Pleasures" or some such. A group of people called sexologists were sitting around talking. As they spoke, they handled and displayed paraphernalia, the tools of their trade, so to speak. They chatted about what male or female body part or orifice one plugs this object into, or puts this item on. One member of the panel proclaimed excitedly that, given the "amazing renewed interest in bondage," easy-to-use devices are now available for binding yourself or your partner. The items in question were black leather cuffs for the wrists and the ankles, for the especially avid pleasure-seeking pair. A handy feature, we were told, was that the cuffs in this device were affixed to a base that, in turn, attached with Velcro to a special bedcover. Thus, if your partner in pleasure, carried away, grew too violent for your taste, you could simply unVelcro yourself. Watching and listening, I admit I was transfixed and somewhat stupified (as I had begun my channel search looking for news or a few scenes from a movie), but I recovered my senses and I asked myself: What would Augustine think of this? What self is here appealed to?

I think he would acknowledge the *delectio* and ask us to ask ourselves what part of the self gets aroused by this sort of thing, and what sort of relationship this arousal, especially if enacted, would habituate us to in relation to ourselves, another person, and the world. What was especially interesting to me, given the presentation of the experts extolling and exhibiting a vast array of instruments of pleasure and torture, was how singularly unappealing they were in their self-pleasing and solemn self-representation. They were the architects of derring-do, they bragged, offering along the way little sermonettes on "casting off inhibition." But what they proposed was all-absorbing, entirely predictable, habituation! Somehow I doubted whether the folks fingering all those "sex tools" and displaying them to the world spent much time thinking about what it means to be a neighbor or tending to the delights of thinking itself. I could be wrong, of course, perhaps they are sexologists by night and Brothers and Sisters of Charity by day, but I doubt it. For these habituating distractions make knowledge of self harder to come by: one hasn't the time or the occasion to pay attention. This would be Augustine's worry, that and what sort of community of mutual predation such people presuppose and require. As he would say, look at what people love, for that is how the self tends.

Knowledge of God

Here I would do well simply to urge all readers of this text to read *De Trinitate*, in part because I don't feel terribly sure-footed in this matter, not being a trained theologian. But I do want to lift up a few points that figure into and bear upon my theme: against the pridefulness of philosophy. Here the central symbol of humbling is, of course, the Cross. If God empties himself and takes on human form and all the troubles of human life, drinking the dregs to the last drop, by what right do we clothe ourselves in pride? This is a theme that runs through Augustine's work, a bright red thread, I am tempted to call it.

Augustine must first shake off his own pride in the high rhetoric he had mastered, in order to "get used to the style in which God's word is spoken," a style that is rough and ready by comparison to the smooth elegance he had once craved.[57] But "the shame" of the Cross is the real scandal to many, that and the "body which he received from a woman. . . ." Such "lowness" is rejected "with disdain" by the lofty because the truth should not come to us in such garb.[58] But only in such garb, generated through love, could God come nearer to us so we could get nearer to him. Humility is a "necessary condition for submission to this truth; and it is no easy task to persuade the proud necks of you philosophers to accept this yoke," then or now.[59]

If, as Dennis Martin reminds us, "at the heart of ancient Christian theory one finds the theme of limitless gift, even to the point of God suffering death by powerlessness (crucifixion), a concept dramatically and ubiquitously symbolized by the crucifix at a level even the simplest mind could grasp, this might have been particularly significant in a culture in which giving and receiving gifts shaped social, political, and economic dynamics."[60] Nowadays, from our pridefulness, we not only "ignore the centrality of kenotic, that is, self-emptying, powerlessness," we—scholars who study the medieval period are those Martin has in mind, but it applies more generally—"unabashedly reinterpret medieval Christian religion in terms of power rather than powerlessness. . . . In short, modern and post-modern assumptions about power and the social construction of reality seriously impair our critical ability to understand medieval men and women."[61] And, I would add, to *read* Augustine, especially in the matter of the self and its relationship to knowledge of a God who is Mediator and himself humiliated.

Christ himself was humble and humbled to the end. "Though the Incarnation of Christ is displeasing to the proud, yet there are also many other things in it which will prove profitable for us to examine and to study."[62] This Christ who is now "preached throughout the world," Augustine reminds an interlocutor, "is not a Christ Who is adorned with an earthly kingdom, nor a Christ rich in earthly possessions, nor a Christ shining with any earthly splendour, but Christ crucified."[63] Even if one humbles oneself in order to come to the Cross, however, there is no guarantee of good fortune by contrast to bad. Faith is not an insurance policy. A hailstorm may take out the crop of the faithful farmer who is kind to his family and good to his neighbors and pass by the farm of the feckless man who ill-treats everyone around him. Nothing can immunize us from ill fortune.

What, in Augustine's arguments against the pridefulness of

philosophy, would commend itself to the nonbeliever, the a- or even anti-theist? There is much: recognition of the extent to which our control over the world is limited; recognition of the fact that human beings live indeterminate and incomplete lives; recognition of the power *exerted over and upon us* by our own habits and memories; recognition of the ways in which the world presses in on all of us, for it is an intractable place where many things go awry and go astray, where one may all-too-easily lose one's very self. The epistemological argument is framed by faith, but it stands on its own as an account of willing, nilling, memory, language, signs, affections, delight, the power and the limits of minds and bodies. To the extent that a prideful philosophy refuses to accept these, Augustine would argue, to that extent philosophy hates the human condition itself. That condition—of particularity, plurality, and commonality—will be the subject of chapter 5, after I take up an important twentieth-century encounter with twentieth-century evil that is framed by Augustine's thought.

4

Augustine's Evil, Arendt's Eichmann

World War II had only just ended. A young Frenchman, who had participated in the resistance and was beginning to make something of a name for himself in literary circles, visited the United States and delivered a lecture at Columbia University in the spring of 1946. Albert Camus struggled to convey something of what he and his compatriots had just suffered through. He spoke of "the human crisis," a "crisis of world-dimensions, a crisis in human consciousness, which I should like now to characterize as clearly as I can." Camus continued:

> What is this crisis, then? I should like—rather than describe it generally—to illustrate it by four brief stories the world is beginning to forget but which still burn in our hearts.
>
> 1). In an apartment rented by the gestapo in a European capital, after a night of questioning, two accused, still bleeding and tightly bound, are discovered; the concierge of the establishment carefully proceeds to set the place in order, her heart light, for she has no doubt breakfasted. Reproached by one of the tortured men, she replies indignantly, "I never mix in the affairs of my tenants."
>
> 2). In Lyon, one of my comrades is taken from his cell for a third examination. In a previous examination his ears had been torn to shreds, and he wears a dressing around his head. The German officer who leads him, the very one who had taken part in the previous interrogation, asks in a tone of affection and solicitude: "How are your ears now?"
>
> 3). In Greece, after an action by the underground forces, a Ger-

man officer is preparing to shoot three brothers he has taken as hostages. The old mother of the three begs for mercy and he consents to spare one of her sons, but on the condition that she herself designate which one. When she is unable to decide, the soldiers get ready to fire. At last she chooses the eldest, because he has a family dependent on him, but by the same token she condemns the two other sons, as the German officer intends.

4). A group of deported women, among whom is one of our comrades, is being repatriated to France by way of Switzerland. Scarcely on Swiss soil, they see a funeral. The mere sight of which causes them to laugh hysterically: "So that is how the dead are treated *here*," they say.[1]

To what was no doubt a hushed auditorium, Camus went on to enumerate the clear symptoms of the crisis. He described them as a rise in terror, following upon such a perversion of values that a man or a historical force is judged today not in terms of human dignity but in terms of success. The crisis is based, as well, on the growing "impossibility of persuasion." Human beings live and can only live by "retaining the idea that they have something in common," a starting point to which they can return.[2] We see, additionally, "the replacement of the natural object by printed matter, by which I mean the growth of bureaucracy." Finally, Camus noted two other symptoms of the crisis. One he called the substitution of the "political" for the "living" person. "For what counts now is whether or not one has helped a doctrine to triumph, not whether or not one respects a mother and spares her suffering."[3] All these symptoms, for Camus, could be summed up in a single tendency—the cult of efficiency and abstraction. "That is why man in Europe today experiences only solitude and silence; for he cannot communicate with his fellows in terms of values common to them all, and since he is no longer protected by a respect for man based on the values of man, the only alternative henceforth open to him is to be a victim or an executioner."[4]

Camus lays the crisis squarely on the doorstep of an unchecked will to power. And from that flows the terrible notion that one can cleanse the world, purge the old, the tired, the imperfect, through terror. Camus argues that politics must be put back in its rightful place, which is a secondary one, and that certain positive values must be affirmed. Taken together, this gestures toward a kind of universalism, a fragile human commonality that is in danger of being lost and that must be struggled for and reaffirmed. Although Camus doesn't label the searing events he depicts, almost laconically; indeed, his matter-of-factness in characterizing what passed for normal life under a system of abnormal terror, clutches the reader as it surely did his audience that day in 1946. What sort of evil is it when it becomes commonplace, everyday, when in *extremis*, for a terrible time, defines the quotidian?

Camus, who had written a dissertation on St. Augustine and neoplatonism, was joined in his attempts to take the measure of what had happened in Europe in mid-century by an American emigré intellectual, Hannah Arendt. In her preface to the first edition of the book that gained her notoriety and international acclaim, *The Origins of Totalitarianism*, Arendt described the final stages of totalitarianism as an "absolute evil." "If it is true that in the final stages of totalitarianism an absolute evil appears (absolute because it can no longer be deduced from comprehensively human motives), it is also true that without it we might never have known the truly radical nature of evil."[5] She leaves the phrase hanging there: but it is a phrase that stuck. When people thought of Nazism, they thought of radical evil. Because she was never a *bien pensant* writer, she also introduced a second theme, one not embraced in the way radical evil was, namely, that the theory "that the Jews are always the scapegoat implies that the scapegoat might well have been anyone else as well. It upholds the perfect innocence of the victim. . . ."[6] Already, in other words, Arendt is striking a blow against reductive Manicheanism in which an external, pervasive evil penetrates, sullies, and destroys a passive (because pure innocence means pure inaction) good.

Arendt wasn't alone in her characterization of totalitarianism as radical evil, of course, but at this juncture she could come up with no other words to capture the horror the world was only then beginning to grapple with. After a time, Nazism was virtually equated with radical evil. Some insisted, then and now, that no other series of events, no other cataclysm in history, deserves to be thus described. Arendt ends her book on totalitarianism with favorite words from Augustine, words promising a new beginning, a new set of possibilities. "Beginning, before it becomes a historical event, is the supreme capacity of man; politically, it is identical with man's freedom. *Initium ut esset homo creatus est*—'that a beginning be made man was created' said Augustine. This beginning is guaranteed by each new birth; it is indeed every man."[7] A book framed by a notion of radical evil ends with an evocation of those human hopes kept alive by the possibility of new beginnings.

Let's move forward a few years. It is 1964 and the publication of Arendt's book *Eichmann in Jerusalem: A Report on the Banality of Evil* has stirred up a hornet's nest.[8] Arendt had covered the Eichmann trial for the *New Yorker* magazine and was struck by Eichmann's sheer thoughtlessness, his apparent inability to utter a word or sentence that wasn't a cliché or a string of clichés, even at the moment of his hanging.[9] He seemed utterly unaware of the nature and magnitude of what he was charged with. In fact, he declared throughout the trial that he had lived according to Kant's moral precepts, especially the definition of duty. Arendt was stunned by the fact that Eichmann came up with "an approximately correct definition of the categorical imperative: 'I meant by my remark about Kant that the principle of my will must always be such that it can become the principle of general laws.'"[10] Eichmann claimed he had read Kant's *Critique of Pure Reason* and had always acted in a way that honored the fact that a law was law and must be obeyed with relentless consistency, even if things sometimes got hard and distasteful. Clearly, weeks of listening to trial testimony and observing the hollow emptiness of Eichmann's reactions had a profound effect on Arendt, so much so that when the time came to end this particular book she wrote as follows: "It was as though in those last minutes he was summing up the lesson that this long course in human wickedness had taught us—the lesson of the fearsome, word-and-thought-defying *banality of evil*."[11] Notes George Kateb: "It may not be radical evil in the Kantian understanding: a Satanic disposition 'to adopt evil *as evil*.' It may not be Milton's Satan saying, 'Evil be thou my Good,' or Claggart in *Billy Budd* tormented by an innocence he must torment. But it may be something altogether more strange: a nonhuman blankness."[12]

With this phrase—the banality of evil—Arendt had unwittingly unleashed a firestorm. She added an Epilogue and then a Postscript to the book in order to try to take account of the controversy it generated. Many members of the Jewish community were wounded by her use of Raul Hildberg's data concerning the role of Jewish Councils in carrying out Nazi dictates and thus themselves becoming part of the infernal machinery of the Final Solution. Arendt insisted, over and over again, that she had never claimed that the Jewish victims of Nazism had acted any differently from anyone else. But she did insist that, even in a situation as horrific as that faced by millions of human souls in Central Europe in the 1940s, there was at least one possibility open: one might have done nothing rather than permitting oneself to get caught up in the process of destruction itself. Of course, those she held to a degree of responsibility were primarily the leaders of the community and not the rank and file of ordinary men and women.

Whatever one's views on the historic data and its interpretation, Arendt's tacit repudiation of her earlier formulation—radical evil—in favor of the banality of evil gives one pause. Whenever we hear or see horrendous wickedness displayed, we search for proper categories to capture our horror. Arendt's subtitle—the banality of evil—suggests that, for Arendt, the phenomenon that stared her in the face at the Jerusalem trial was quite simply this: Eichmann was neither Iago nor MacBeth. "Except for an extraordinary diligence in looking out for his personal advancement, he had no motives at all." He was not, she averred, stupid. It was something else—"sheer thoughtlessness—that predisposed him to become one of the greatest criminals of that period. And if this is 'banal' and even funny, if with the best will in the world one cannnot extract any diabolical or demonic profundity from Eichmann, that is still far from calling it commonplace."[13] She would deprive evil of its seductive power; indeed, she proclaimed it one of her purposes: "To destroy the legend of the greatness of evil, of the demonic force, to take away from people the admiration they have for great evil-doers like Richard III."[14]

There is, Arendt concludes, a strange interdependence of thoughtlessness and evil. In fact, it is far easier for us to imagine a grandeur of evil and to make the monsters and masters of evil demonic, hence attractive demiurges, than to take the measure of their dreadful ordinariness, of what had become, in an extreme time and place in the recent past, commonplace: the way we now do things around here. Consider our own continuing fascination with the Nazis and Nazism. Week after week on television, dramas and documentaries proclaim the uniquely absorbing evil mentality and daring, if monstrous, deeds of the "gangster clique" that ran the Third Reich. Hitler, Goebbels, Goering, Himmler—the lot—are held out or held up as the embodiment of evil, as the progenitors of a kind of negative anti-creation, a demonic urgency that exercises its own fatal attraction on some, even as it titillates many. It was this that Arendt was trying to undermine.

She writes:

> It would have been very comforting indeed to believe that Eichmann was a monster. . . . the trouble with Eichmann was precisely

that so many were like him, and that the many were neither perverted nor sadistic, that they were and still are terribly and terrifyingly normal. From the viewpoint of our legal institutions and of our moral standards of judgement, this normality was much more terrifying than all the atrocities put together, for it implied that this new type of criminal, who is in actual fact *hostis generis humani,* commits his crimes under circumstances that make it well nigh impossible for him to know or to feel that he is doing wrong.[15]

It seems to be very difficult to pin down Arendt here. Surely evil, even in its most banal form, cannot simply be a matter of thoughtlessness: our minds rebel at this thought. But Arendt insists that there are no lofty words to describe the phenomena she dissects, at times almost clinically. For her, it was a matter of what she called "factual truth." Her earlier use of the category— radical evil—had missed the boat in critical ways. What one sees, in Eichmann, in Nazism as a mass phenomenon, in the implementation of the final solution, is instead a privation, something diminished, tawdry, uncompelling. Arendt aims to strip the Nazis of their demiurgic standing, hence their power to draw us to them as if they, and their stormtroopers in gleaming black boots, had poured forth from the portals of hell itself. For this image exerts a deadly and seductive attraction.

For her pains, Arendt was greeted with harsh criticism, even denunciation. She was accused of insufficient love for her own people; indeed, of blaming the Jewish people for their fate under Nazism. Shaken as she was by these criticisms, Arendt fought back. She reaffirmed that there are differences in degree of responsibility and culpability for outcomes. Although there may not have been a possibility for active revolt against Nazi policies, including mass shipments, deportations, and killings, one might have resisted by doing nothing, by refusing to comply. She clung to this narrow band of responsibility *in situ,* as it were, but unenacted, as if to a tensile strand. She labored to tease out the fragile and narrow ground between seeing the Jewish people as an

undifferentiated category of victims (much the way the Nazis
saw them) or, alternatively, seeing them caught in the maw of the
most hideous infernal political machine the world had seen,
with some actively fighting back, others fleeing, and others trag-
ically complying with orders in the hope that over the long run
a "saving remnant" would remain to tell the story. But she re-
fused to relent in the matter of the banality of evil.

In an acrimonious exchange with Gershom Scholem, she
writes:

> You are quite right: I changed my mind and do no longer speak of
> "radical evil." It is a long time since we last met, or we would per-
> haps have spoken about the subject before. (Incidentally, I don't see
> why you call my term "banality of evil" a catchword or slogan. As
> far as I know no one has used the term before me; but that is unim-
> portant.) [But, as we shall see, she had a forefather pushing her this
> direction.] It is indeed my opinion now that evil is never "radical,"
> that it is only extreme, and that it possesses neither depth nor any
> demonic dimension. It can overgrow and lay waste the whole world
> precisely because it spreads like a fungus on the surface. It is
> "thought-defying," as I said, because thought tries to reach some
> depth, to go to the roots, and the moment it concerns itself with evil,
> it is frustrated because there is nothing. That is its "banality." Only
> the good has depth and can be radical.[16]

Augustine's Evil

Consider Arendt's words: Evil is banal. It lacks depth. It has no
standing on its own. It doesn't qualify as sin in the context of a
good creation. In order to sin one must face temptation and
delectation and offer some kind of assent. There is a struggle
and finally an assent of the will. But evil is a surd. It signifies
nothing. It is no-thing. It is a flattening of the world through a
failure to engage it. Thought- and world-defying, in Arendt's
phrase. Nill. Nihil. Here Hannah Arendt, as elsewhere, is Augus-

tine's faithful daughter. To capture the depth of her horror at the era through which she has lived, she returns to one of her first great teachers, St. Augustine. It is surprising to me that, at this late date, no one, to my knowledge, in that vast cottage industry that is Arendt studies has made the connection—one apparent to this reader of Augustine—between Arendt's banality of evil and Augustine's metaphysical construction of evil in relation to good.

Augustine's long struggle with understanding sin and the relation of sin to evil is the story of his struggle with Manicheanism. We must return to *The Confessions*, then, for an account that aims to lay bare Augustine's recognition that evil is not a free-standing active principle of anticreation but, instead, a privation, a diminution.[17] Contrary to the view of evil as an active, polluting force before which good is essentially passive—the Manichean view Augustine had once accepted but had struggled his way out of because he could "make no progress" in understanding evil within this Manichean metaphysic—evil, for Augustine, lost its allure. Evil is something each person has to grapple internally with because, in fact, no external force, no devil makes one do it. If we take the measure of the theory of evil Augustine rejected, we can see something of that flattened wasteland Arendt glimpsed listening to Eichmann spout clichés more than a thousand years later.

As a child, Augustine is caught up in a world of forbidden desires and pleasures. He loves the wrong things. There is temptation and delight and all too often consent—sin, in other words. Early on, however, he makes other observations. He begins to discern the importance of representations and mimesis; thus, unchaste love is a flawed human enactment, a kind of pallid mimesis, of God's love and fecundity. Despite these moments of reckoning, all Augustine succeeds in doing for years is to create of himself a "barren waste."[18] He feels flat, empty, sterile. He encounters a theater of cruelty and asks, Why do we enjoy watching the misery of others? If pity were genuine, it would prefer that there be no cause, as my pleasure in my reaction turns on the misery of others. When he makes his first conversion to philosophy, on the trail of earthly wisdom, and, at the urging of his mother, opens the Christian Scriptures, he encounters his own strong resistance. His engagement with the Christian Scriptures is a failure, an aesthetic disappointment, and a philosophical letdown. He finds the rhetoric simplistic and clumsy by contrast to the stately prose of Cicero and the elegant emanations of neoplatonism.[19] He hears a Manichean speaker proclaiming "Truth! Truth!" and because he is hungry, so he eats. But he is not satisfied. In fact, the more he eats the more he starves.

We know the story of his fitful movement of self through the moment in the garden. He opens and reads, and the rest, as they say, is history. But let's step back to the travails en route and consider the way in which he introduces evil as the privation of good in *The Confessions*, Book III. He writes of his attraction for the Manicheans and their teachings. Yet he perceives that he is falling further away from the truth. "I did not know that evil is nothing but the removal of good until finally no good remains. How could I see this when, with the sight of my eyes, I saw no more than material things and with the sight of my mind no more than their images?"[20] Still he hung in there with the Manicheans for a while, trying to come to grips with the idea that God was somehow dispersed and that there were little God particles scattered throughout the universe. "Anything which anyone treads underfoot would be a part of God! In the killing of any living creature, a part of God would be slaughtered! I shrink from uttering all the possibilities which come to mind; it would be impossible to mention them without shame."[21] An alternative evil principle is similarly diffused, making its home in matter, in that which is polluted. Augustine tries to make this dualism do. He wants a tidy world/antiworld, if he can get it, a world in which perfect good squares off against perfect evil. This was handy, this Manichean construal, because when things went wrong he could blame the flesh as the principle of evil: matter polluted and was polluting, but the purity of spirit was unscathed. Yet it was his soul, his very self, that felt empty even though, ostensibly, its purity was not struck, despite the body's doings.

Finally, when he has a chance to encounter a great Manichean teacher, the famed Faustus, face to face, Augustine is disappointed. Faustus makes all sorts of dogmatic claims, many based on epistemological privilege, that stir up Augustine's suspicions and cannot meet his ardent challenges, especially his continuing torment about the problem of evil. Augustine observes the pride that solidifies when evil can be sloughed off into a separate category—whether in that flesh that is not essentially part of me, or as the burden of the impure followers in the Manichean community—the apprentices who are not yet members of the Manichean elect and are therefore assigned the dirty work, for example, plucking fruit and "other acts of violence."[22] Finally, it hits him: we can no longer claim that it is not we who sin but some other nature that sins within us. "It flattered my pride to think that I incurred no guilt, and when I did wrong, not to confess it so that you might bring healing to a soul that had sinned against you. I preferred to excuse myself and blame this unknown thing that was in me but was not part of me. The truth, of course, was that it was all my own self and my own impiety had divided me against myself. My sin was all the more incurable because I did not think myself a sinner."[23]

From that point on, Augustine understands evil differently: remember, he is grappling not just with the commission of sin by individuals but with the whole story of creation by a good God. He rejects the notion that God created evil as a full-fledged malignant principle, as he had once imagined or been compelled to believe. "For, ignorant as I was, I thought of evil not as some vague substance but as an actual bodily substance, and this was because I could not conceive of mind except as a rarified body somehow diffused in space."[24] When he confronts the Manichees with his new arguments, their responses are weak. Rather than arguing out the point, they retreat to dogmatic reassertion of what, for Augustine, had become dubious claims that offer an

inadequate creation account and fuel self-exculpation and satis-
faction. Disabused, Augustine forges forth on his own until,
through complex modes of figurative and textual exegesis, he
finds that he can, once again, make progress in his quest to understand and to offer a compelling account of that which vexes
him: Who and what is our God? What is goodness? What is my
relation to created being? What sort of creature am I? How am I
responsible for turning a body that is good into a slave of bad
habits? What is this thing we name evil?

Finally, having rejected the notion that God is a bodily substance extended in space, Augustine gives up on the Manichees,
who, he argues, deceive both themselves and others. For all their
talk, he writes scathingly, they are no better than "mutes," for it
"was not your holy Word which spoke from their lips."[25] A primary sacrilege they committed, according to Augustine, was "I
could still not find a clear explanation, without complications, of
the cause of evil. Whatever the cause might be I saw that it was
not to be found in any theory that would oblige me to believe
that the immutable God was mutable." He now makes philosophic progress, realizing that when I choose to do something or
not to do it, it is my own self that wills to sin or refrains from
sinning. For the Manichees, God suffers evil; for the Augustinian
Christian the human person, from free will, commits a sin and
partakes of that dearth we name evil. This is too pat as stated, of
course, but it puts things squarely on human shoulders. We are
the ones who perpetrate. God neither suffers evil to be done, nor
does he create wickedness in order to stir up a cataclysmic metaphysical battle between the forces of good and forces of evil,
what might be called the Star Wars scenario. In this new Augustinian scheme of things, evil is denuded, stripped of its glory, depleted. Evil is the name we give to an assent to temptation that
congeals into thoughtless habituation and a chain of servitude.
This habituation, this chain of servility, must be broken up if we
are to think and act clearly.

Evil Unmasked But Not Unchained

Evil, then, is not incarnated; it is not an entity brought into being by God, whether through generation or in God's suffering it to emerge. Evil is the unbearable lightness of nonbeing. The Devil and the bad angels, in Augustine's delightful—if such a solemn topic can fairly be said to delight—account in *The City of God*, are without bodies. They do not know what it is like to be in the world in incarnate form. In fact, they spend a lot of time roaming around seeking modes of representation. They search for something they can attach themselves to, so to speak, so that they might appear in the world through surrogates, in a secondhand kind of way, a B-movie, if you will.[26] "The demon attached to an image by an impious art," Augustine writes, "has been made a god by man, but a god for this particular kind of man, not for all mankind."[27] Disembodied, the devil's minions are not only the mascots of thoughtlessness, they are the loathers of created life. The story goes like this—and it is, I believe, one compelling way to account for Arendt's choice of the banality of evil to name Nazism. God created the world and saw that it was good. It must needs be good because God is the fullness of good, the plenitude and absolute and immutable good. Goodness cannot generate evil, for that would mean that goodness somehow partakes of evil. It follows that evil does not emerge through an act of generation. It is not created. Rather, evil is a kind of noncreation, a draining away from that which is. "The loss of good has been given the name of 'evil,'" Augustine writes in Book XI, chapter 9, of *The City of God*.[28]

If one held that evil was created, then who is the creative and generative force behind it? If one accepts this account, one is in a universe replete with a pantheon of dark and cunning evil deities telling evil deed doers, in effect: "I like what I see; go forth and kill again." If evil were generative, one would have to hold that evil is embodied; that matter is the work of an evil demiurge; and that evil has generative power. What, then, does one make of

"John's statement about the Devil, that 'he is a sinner from the beginning'. . ."? Augustine responds that John himself gives the answer. It is a "baneful teaching" to assume that "the Devil has evil as the essential principle of his being, that his nature derives from some hostile First Principle."[29] Rather, the matter is one not of *nature* but of sinning, of commission, not essence. Indeed, the *choice* of evil "is an impressive proof that the *nature* is good."[30] If the evil were in, or were, the nature, no choice would be necessary in order for evil to manifest itself.

By contrast, in Manichean dualism, an evil demiurge creates matter as a defiling essence that is not, however, the essence of man, essentially defined as he is by spirit, by nonmatter. In this scheme of things, God becomes a kind of magnet who tries to draw the good to himself. Evil, in this scenario, flows from a powerful antithetical demiurge, more or less coequal with God but taking an eternal walk on the wild side. Now, mind you, God himself loves antitheses, Augustine notes: they are part of the world's beauty. God enriches "the course of the world history by the kind of antithesis which gives beauty to a poem. 'Antithesis' provides the most attractive figures in literary composition: the Latin equivalent is 'opposition,' or, more accurately, 'contra-position'. . . . The opposition of such contraries gives an added beauty to speech; and in the same way there is beauty in the composition of the world's history arising from the antithesis of contraries—a kind of eloquence in events, instead of in words."[31] God takes pleasure in contrasts, then, but that does not usher into metaphysical dualism.

Consider the different picture drawn in Augustine's mature metaphysic. God is generative. He created the world and it was good. Evil represents a falling away. "The truth is that one should not try to find an efficient cause for a wrong choice. It is not a matter of efficiency, but of deficiency; the evil will itself is not effective but defective."[32] Man is the agent of this falling away, not because the body is corrupt, but because we can defile it. "There is no such entity in nature as 'evil'; 'evil' is merely a name for the privation of good."[33] Evil is the turning of a limited creature from God to himself and, hence, to an absolutizing of his own flawed will "which has become habitual, and has developed and hardened into 'second nature'. . . ."[34] We become clichéd. We repeat. Nothing new emerges. We are on automatic pilot. We think we are free agents and yet we are trammeled and traduced. For "evil things cannot exist without the good, since the natural entities in which evil exists are certainly good, in so far as they are natural."[35] Thrown back on the presumption that we creatures in finitude can constitute ourselves as the Selfsame, we sadly offer evidence that we cannot even generate a principle of evil alterity; we can at best perpetrate, through willing-nilling, the depletion of that which is good.

Stripping evil of its power in this way is no small accomplishment and it is a very difficult one. In fact, look around you. Does not our popular culture embody evil as an active principle, having force of its own, caught in a coequal battle with the forces of good? It is difficult to get out of this dualistic way of thinking. Christians remain indebted to it although it is at odds with their own theology of creation. Remember Augustine's words from Book XI, chapter 22 of *The City of God*: "There is no such entity in nature as evil. Evil is merely a name for the privation of good." This is one of Augustine's many Wittgensteinian moves— or, perhaps better put, Wittgenstein made many Augustinian moves—calling 'evil' the 'name' we conventionally give to a class of acts and putative motives. Our problem, and tendency, has been to read back from the deed or imputed motive to what might be called an anticreation, a negative of the self, even the universe. "There is a scale of values stretching from earthly to heavenly realities, from the visible to the invisible; and the inequality between these goods makes possible the existence of them all. Now God is the great artificer in the great things; but that does not mean that he is an inferior artist in the small."[36]

Augustine's most intriguing account of evil, as I have already

indicated, is found in Book XII of *The City of God*, the point at
which a limited creature turns from God to himself and becomes
a principle of nullity as a result. Remembering that good and bad
angels have the same nature, it helps us to make sense of the enmity to God, the hatred of finitude, the loathing of creatureliness
itself that is so central to what we name as evil. Even the fact that
no one, neither angels nor human beings, is punished for a fault
of nature but, rather for faults of willing, often invites violent
chagrin: it would be so much easier to blame one's nature, to see
oneself as the passive conduit through which evil enacts and em-
anates. It would be utterly wrong to have any doubt about this,
Augustine avers, since God created the world of stuff, that world
that is "so full of a number of things / I'm sure we should all be
as happy as kings." Enmity toward God is enmity toward the
world itself and this enmity comports with self-pride. Indeed,
the roundelay of sin is pride: the self becomes the standpoint of
itself. If there is no point of reference outside the self, over time
what emerges is a deficiency as, through habituation, the self is
further depleted. Once again, we hear a tale of loss; we confront
a sense of depletion, of thoughtlessness, rather than standing in
terrible wonder before something grand that inspires a shudder
of desire in all who witness it.

Listening to the stories of survivors in the Jerusalem trial, witness to the millions who died ignominiously in Nazi camps,
Hannah Arendt was determined not to permit Eichmann or any
like him to attain the stature of dramatic or romantic demiurges;
no, these were limited, hollowed-out, pale and empty men. This
was the banality of evil. In his novel *An Admirable Woman*, Arthur
Cohen puts words into the mouth of his Jewish emigré American intellectual protagonist, Erika Hertz:

> I was not going to fall victim to the charge of Burckhardt that con-
> temporaries refuse to be historical about their own history because
> they falsely imagine that their age is the summation and triumph of
> historical processes that have been bubbling through time's caverns

for centuries. I knew the opposite. My age—yours and mine—is no summation, much less a triumph. Quite the contrary. Ours, if anything, is a nadir, and not even that. It is an age that has demonstrated more wildly than any other what happens when the state consorts with its industry and military to secure power and together delude themselves into believing they can hold it forever.[37]

The flesh and blood woman on whom Erika Hertz was based had this to say after recounting the terrible story of the banality of evil: "under some conditions of terror most people will comply but *some people will not*, just as the lesson of the countries to which the Final Solution was proposed is that 'it could happen' in most places *but it did not happen everywhere*. Humanly speaking, no more is required, and no more can reasonably be asked, for this planet to remain a fit place for human habitation."[38]

I daresay that Arendt's companion in thought, Augustine, would agree with this sober and poignant conclusion. If, then, you would understand the banality of evil, you must have some sense of Augustine's grappling with the question of evil and his own brave and brilliant move—indebted to neoplatonism, to be sure—to strip it of any suggestion of generative power. This is a point worth belaboring. The possibility of bringing something new into being is the name Arendt gives to action. But surely, many will argue, Arendt herself declares that one of the horrors of totalitarianism is precisely the fact that, introduced into the world, it may happen again. Doesn't this make of totalitarianism a moment of newness, of generative power?

The answer is "no." The reason, as I can best articulate it, goes like this. Let's say that something horrific appears for the first time: Vlad the Impaler introduces a novelty as he starts to impale people and no one has ever been impaled before. (I am not making this as a historically accurate claim about Vlad the Impaler. For all I know he merely perfected what others had begun, but that isn't central to my point.) This new point of evil can only repeat itself: it rapidly falls into mimesis, repetition, thoughtless habituation. The resolute impaler must try to stomp out any other possibility of newness, so to speak, for his regime turns on successful impalings. The process becomes automatic—the way we do things around here. I am suggesting that an event may be *novel* without being *generative*.[39]

To be sure, this gets tricky when one confronts evil master minds like Hitler or Stalin. Arendt apparently wants us to see these initiators of a chain of terrible events as banal, too. I think one can make this work by reminding oneself of what happens when an individual is in the grip of an ideology, an architectonic scheme, a "genocidal fantasy," in Kateb's words.[40] Evil cannot permit the space for the unexpected to happen. Totalitarian evil must try to take up all the available space; must work to destroy all the living tissue of social life and civil society. This is the work of ideology. Good, by contrast, cannot be thus initiated and, if you will, *planned*, because it relies on the unrehearsed deed-doing of ordinary men and women who, from time to time, are capable of the extraordinary act, like the villagers of Le Chambon depicted in Philip Hallie's wonderful book *Lest Innocent Blood Be Shed*.[41] Their death-defying acts of rescue and asylum for refugees from Nazi terror were generative, radiating out, opening up new possibilities for decency. Their goodness flowed from habit or character, not thoughtless habituation. This is a subtle but big difference. Generativity or mimesis, that is the question.

When Arendt revisited the theme of the banality of evil for the last time before her death, in her posthumously published *Life of the Mind*, she wrote:

> However, what I was confronted with was utterly different and still undeniably factual. I was struck by a manifest shallowness in the doer that made it impossible to trace the incontestable evil of his deeds to any deeper level of roots or motives. The deeds were monstrous, but the doer—at least the very effective one now on trial—was quite ordinary, commonplace, and neither demonic nor monstrous. . . . it was not stupidity but *thoughtlessness*. . . . Clichés, stock phrases, adher-

ence to conventional, standardized codes of expression and conduct have the socially recognized function of protecting us against reality, that is, against the claim on our thinking attention that all events and facts make by virtue of their existence. . . . It was this absence of thinking—which is so ordinary an experience in our everyday life, where we have hardly the time, let alone the inclination, to *stop* and think—that awakened my interest.[42]

— 5 —

"Our business within this
common mortal life": Augustine
and a Politics of Limits

Love may not be all you need. But, whether as the yearnings prompted by *caritas* or those pale enactments spurred by *cupiditas*, love is a dominant theme within our common mortal life. Augustine was in love with the world, a world he called "a smiling place."[1] His biographer tells us he loved the world "immoderately," and one senses the truth of this. Only someone caught up in a love affair with the world would describe so deliciously its many delectations and articulate so artfuly its temptations. Peace and hope are twin possibilities that emerge from all our yearnings and longings, holy and otherwise. But peace in its true form as harmony and righteousness is not attainable on this earth, although the hope that keeps alive our longing for it is what stands between us and that emptiness of the abyss, that flatness of being Augustine credited as the work of sin and the fruit of deformed willing. Even in our good works we are dislocated creatures, torn by discord, but striving to attain some measure of *concordia*.[2] But love abides. And the more we try to emulate God's love, the stronger will be our hope; the more decent our lives with and among one another.

> Love, then, is not expended like money, for in addition to the fact that money is diminished by expenditure and love is increased, they differ in this too, that we give greater evidence of good-will towards anyone if we do not seek the return of money we have given him; whereas no one can sincerely expend love unless he insist on being repaid; for when money is received, it is so much gain to the recip-

ient but so much loss to the donor; love, on the other hand, is not
only augmented in the man who demands it back from the person
he loves, even when he does not receive it, but the person who returns it actually begins to possess it only when he pays it back.[3]

This is more complex by far than 'what goes around comes
around.' It is a story of increase through apparent (but only apparent) depletion. It is not a sentimental tale; not, one might say,
a project that yields treacle for a greeting card. It is a discipline
that creates a self. Better put, the self emerges only through this
discipline, this project of reciprocity that includes demands. As
we shall see, Augustine, here as elsewhere, does not offer a program or a plan. He strenuously repudiates utopian possibilities
and, from Plato's republic to Rousseau's polity, to Marx's classless
society, to Mill's happy ordering of liberal choosers, we in the
West have enshrined thinkers who promised to remove obstacles
to the good life, or who assured us that such obstacles were, in
principle, removable. It has been a fantasy of (some) philosophers, from antiquity to modernity, that the barriers that appear
to stand in the way of instantiating in practice an abstract theoretical understanding would one day fall or simply melt down in
the light of transformed ratiocination, or a sufficient application
of political will, or an overthrow of the rotten practices of the
old order, or 'reeducating' those who go around planting 'Stop'
or 'Proceed with Caution' signs all over the human landscape.

For example, one variant on the Marxist project was an odd
combination of deep cynicism about the present, with its distorted relations, consciousness, and practices, by contrast to a future moment within an emancipated human community. In that
historic epiphany, boundaries and tensions would have melted
away and a oneness or harmony—species-being—would have
triumphed. The individual would be at one with himself or herself as well as the species entire; the social order would be cured
of all its previous dissensions, conflicts, and divisions. Augustine
offers no such assurances. He knows that dreams of this sort die

hard and that the notion of positive transcendence of estrangement will always beckon. But we should resist its allure, the better to serve, not to ignore, our neighbor.

What does Augustine offer, by contrast? It is a *via negativa*, above all. By that I mean: Augustine displays the negative of ideology by articulating a canny and scrupulous attunement to the here and now with its very real limits. There *are* affirmations that flow from his negation of positive philosophy. Augustine creates a complex moral map that offers space for loyalty and love and care, as well as for a chastened form of civic virtue. If Augustine is a thorn in the side of those who would cure the universe once and for all, he similarly torments cynics who disdain any project of human community, or justice, or possibility. We time-bound creatures, doomed or compelled to narrate our lives within temporality, within what Augustine calls the *saeculum*, can gather together the self and forge a compelling if not conflict-free identity. Wisdom comes from experiencing fully the ambivalence and ambiguity that is the human condition. This is what Augustine called our business "within this common mortal life," and any politics that disdains this business, this caring for the quotidian, is a dangerous or misguided or misplaced politics.

Human affairs, as I have already argued, are murky and bound to remain so. Earthly time is not subject to a progressivist teleology or reading. At one time we will be in the end-time, but in the meantime we cannot entertain hopes of anything that can reasonably be called sure and certain progress—change, yes, but continuing transformation toward some preformed ideal, no. Augustine believed, as many Augustinian scholars have observed, that he had uncovered the lowest common denominators of human existence in the *saeculum*: a need for social life, hence for peace and order; a divided will easily traduced by a lust to dominate and to possess; a world of insoluble estrangements, perils, and shortcomings. But this was a man who loved and hoped. "Give me a man in love: he knows what I mean. Give me one who yearns; give me one who is hungry; give me one far away in

this desert, who is thirsty and sighs for the spring of the Eternal
country. Give me that sort of man: he knows what I mean. But if
I speak to a cold man, he just does not know what I am talking
about. . . ."[4] Let's see if we can sort this out.

The Two Cities, Yet Again

The theme of the two cities, as I have already indicated, lies at the
heart of Augustine's alternative to worshiping at the altar of the
earthly city; to absolutizing our temporary arrangements. From
John Neville Figgis's early classic; through more recent, superb
treatments—here I am thinking of Robert Markus's *Saeculum*, and
John Milbank's *Theology and Social Theory*—what Augustine hoped
to do with his characterization of the two cities figures centrally
in all treatments of his work, especially those that aim to sort out
what Augustine has to do with, or for, any current political project. For Figgis, the *civitas terrena* is a story of all earthly cities (up
to Augustine's own point in time), from Assyria through Rome.
Peace is the theme or goal of the earthly city, but it is all too often
a peace achieved through harsh conquest and dominion, hence
no real peace at all. That peace is reserved for the *civitas dei* and its
pax aeterna; however, Figgis suggests that Augustine begins to
"identify *Civitas Dei* with the Church."[5]

Markus does not agree with this latter formulation. Just as
Augustine repudiates the theology underscoring the notion of an
imperium Christianum—coming, as he does, to regard the "Chris-
tianization of the empire as illusory," he similarly refuses to conflate *civitas dei* and church. Markus is insistent, and persuasive,
that it is not at all surprising that Augustine initially succumbed
to the notion of a Christian empire. But, he argues, what we need
to understand is "why he, almost alone among his contemporaries, managed to break the spell."[6] The achievements of the
earthly city are "radically infected with the ambiguity of all
human achievement." Although earthly institutions "have a real
claim upon men," they cannot brand as their own the entirety of

us, for true fulfillment is reserved for the heavenly city.[7] As Augustine moves further away from what Markus calls his "classical starting point," his hopes and aspirations for human society diminish, but not to the vanishing point, as we shall see.

John Milbank throws down the gauntlet in a provocative way in his quest for a "true Christian metanarrative realism." If that is what one is about, then one "must attempt to retrieve and elaborate the account of history given by Augustine in *Civitas Dei*."[8] And that is a very particular tale of two cities. Indeed,

> from a postmodern perspective, Augustine's philosophy of history appears more viable than that of either Hegel or Marx. These two provide 'gnostic' versions of Augustine's critical Christianity by giving us a story in which antagonism is inevitably brought to an end by a necessary dialectical passage through conflict. Augustine, on the other hand, puts peaceful reconciliation in no dialectical relationship with conflict . . . but rather does something prodigiously more historicist, in that he isolates the codes which support the universal sway of antagonism, and contrasts this with the code of a peaceful mode of existence, which has historically arisen as 'something else', an *altera civitas*, having no logical or causal connection with the city of violence.[9]

For Milbank, what Augustine achieves is nothing less than an immanent critique "or deconstruction of antique political society."

I have already noted that the earthly city is inescapably marked by sin. This means many things and I have discussed a few: the quest for insular self-esteem and self-aggrandizement; an urge to dominate over others, to be a self only in relation as a master to a slave, or as a slave who would be master; an urgency toward order that all too readily slides over into the massive dis-order of a coercive *imperium*. But this just scratches the surface. Let's dig a little deeper. We need to begin with Augustine's starting point, his presumptive launching pad. We start with, and in, the *saeculum*, the name for that temporal period between the Fall and the end-time; that sphere within which we are "pressed" and in which our range of action is real but limited.

Augustine repudiates stories of mythical beginnings that presume disorder, with the founders of cities or republics or empires cast as the bringers of order.[10] Take Hobbes, for example. One starts with a terrible disorder. Only the *Leviathan* can cure this one: bring in the Behemoth! Freud tells his story of origins as one in which the frightful and all-powerful primal father is killed and eaten by the resentful sons—then and only then can a brotherhood and a sense of justice emerge in the band, plus a pretty heavy quotient of guilt and remorse at having killed the old man, repugnant as was his absolute dominion. Violence is pitted against violence. Augustine agrees that the earthly city is "marked" or "stained" by sin. But this sin should usher into a rueful recognition of limits, not a will to dominion that requires others for one to conquer.[11] If one starts one's story by positing an ontology of violence, it is difficult, if not impossible, to get away from the implication that we are in a dog-eat-dog or, if we want to be fair to dogs, a master-eat-slave-eat-master world.

Where, then, does Augustine begin? With the presumption of peace and its priority over war, over conflict emerging from the *libido dominandi*. This peace is attained fitfully in the *altera civitas* in its earthly pilgrimage; haphazardly, at best, in all earthly cities; and in its full richness only in the city of God, when the time of pressing for the human race in temporality comes to an end. Different understandings of power are at work here. There is the power of earthly dominion—*potestas*—but there are other forms of power, forms that are generative, not controlling—that are exemplified most fully in God's power to generate a world that he then so loved "he gave his only begotten Son" to save a fitful and frail humanity. Because earthly *potestas* is tied to the temptations inherent to that form of power we call *dominion*, there can be no such thing as an earthly sacral society or state. God forbid we should sacralize our earthly arrangements in this way! (Clearly, Augustine would have a thing or two to say to those folks who equate America with a sacral order. This is not "God's country," Augustine would surely say, but yet another nation "under God's judgment.")

But let's turn to Augustine himself, at long last. He begins to unpack "the origins and ends of the two cities" in *The City of God*, Part II, Book XI. A "poverty-stricken kind of power" characterizes the earthly city. Like the fallen angels, human beings turn away from God. And that turning away gets crystallized, as it were, into various earthly arrangements. Augustine continues the theme of "turning away" or evil in Book XII, tying the two cities to "wills and desires." With Book XIV we get the disobedience of the first man leading, not to death everlasting as would have been the case without God's grace, but to division—within the self, between self and other, between nations and cultures. But whatever the culture or nation, none is whole unto itself, complete and perfect; each is marked by the divisions Augustine here calls "the standard of the flesh" by contrast to the "standard of the spirit."[12] Remember that this is not a screed against the body or embodiment but against what Augustine takes to be the misuse or abuse of the body on, or under, the rule of the flesh.

With Book XV he writes of "two classes" or "two cities, speaking allegorically," a warning to any who would conflate specific earthly configurations with his dominant metaphor. It is an "allegorical representation" of a "great mystery." The clean and the unclean come together within the framework of the Church, within the boundaries of human communities.[13] But the city of God is turned toward God's will, with which it hopes to be in accord; the city of man is according to man's standards and designs. Given that there is a "darkness that attends the life of human society," few should sit comfortably on "the judge's bench . . ." But sit there the judge must, "for the claims of human society constrain him and draw him to this duty; and it is unthinkable to him that he should shirk it," but he must needs sit uneasily.[14]

Living an earthly life, what rules should one follow? What is one to do? Temporal peace is a good, whether it is the peace of the body (health and soundness), or fellowship with one's own kind, or "light, speech, air to breathe, water to drink, and whatever is suitable for the feeding and clothing of the body, for the care of the body and the adornment of the person."[15] Amidst the shadows that hover over, above, among, there are nonetheless two rules we can follow: "first, to do no harm to anyone, and, secondly, to help everyone whenever possible."[16] This is the ethic of the pilgrim; of the one who is tethered to this earth and its arrangements through bonds of affection and necessity but who recognizes at the same time that these arrangements are not absolute and not final.

Just as the household is a component part that contributes to the completeness of the whole, so our work in small ways and about small things, contributes to the overall harshness or decency of any social order. On this earth there must be compromises "between human wills" if there is to be anything resembling peace; indeed, the heavenly city on pilgrimage helps to forge peace by calling out "citizens from all nations and so collects a society of aliens, speaking all languages." She—the *civitas dei*—does not annul or abolish earthly differences but even "maintains them and follows them," so long as God can be worshiped; in this way, she makes "use of the earthly peace" and it is in her interest, as we might now say, to help to contribute to earthly peace.[17] The life of the saint, like the life of the citizen, is a social life. We are with, and among, one another. There must be a balance in our attention to earthly affairs; thus, a person ought not "to be so leisured as to take no thought in that leisure for the interest of his neighbour, nor so active as to feel no need for the contemplation of God." If we are to "promote the well-being of the common people," we must love God and love our neighbor, and the one helps to underscore and animate the other.[18]

We return, then, to the definition of a commonwealth. This is worth one more pass. The problem with the definition advanced by Scipio in Cicero's *On the Republic*, remember, is its penury, its conclusion that a people is "a multitude 'united in association by a common sense of right and a community of interest.'"[19] This does not suffice, as I argued in chapter 2 above, and even if it did, on this definition alone, inadequate as it is, Rome was not a true commonwealth. Rome was dominated by the interest of the stronger and this is a "false conception" of justice. Cicero makes a "vigorous and powerful argument on behalf of justice against injustice," but if one ardently seeks justice, one requires a more expansive set of human possibilities that simultaneously humble us, yet draw us into care for our earthly city. For our ties to the earthly city are strong, resilient, tenacious.

This is where love comes in—love of God and love of neighbor—and this is where justice enters as well. Augustine's alternative definition starts with love. "A people is the association of a multitude of rational beings united by a common agreement on the objects of their love." It "follows that to observe the character of a particular people we must examine the objects of its love."[20] No single man can create a commonwealth. There is no ur-Founder, no great bringer of order. It begins in ties of fellowship, in households, clans, and tribes, in earthly love and its many discontents. And it begins in an ontology of peace, not war.

What has Augustine here accomplished with his allegorical play of the two cities? Given Augustine's emphasis on *pax* and his devastating send-up of the Roman *imperium*, some (notably Figgis) have argued that if there is a set of earthly arrangements he would favor, it would be something like a League of Nations, an international comity consisting of small states, somewhat comparable to the households of a city. If this sounds naive, it is a naivete shared by many among our great twentieth-century civic actors, including Jane Addams, who found in the comingling of many nations within the great American cities at the turn of the century, a kind of template or image of what a (relatively) peaceful earthly dominion, global in scope, might be. Augustine, of course, spent far more time plumbing our heart of darkness than did Addams, but it is interesting that they emerge at roughly the same place from time to time—working with analogies, trying to find a thread through the no-man's-land of war and empire.

Markus credits Augustine with dropping the whole idea of an *imperium Christianum* and the theology attendant upon it, as I noted above. But more should be added and it is a critical note Markus here inserts. It would seem that, given his knocking away the props that serve to justify dominant forms of earthly coercion, and his repudiation of the Theodosian establishment, Augustine might have "opened the door to the non-coercive exercise of office, pastoral and political," but he never makes this latter move; hence, his repudiation of coercion by the Church of unbelievers, combined with an insistence that coercion is a necessary, if regrettable, feature within the community of believers.[21] One might respond to Markus in this way—and it isn't to justify Augustine's acceptance of the occasional need for coercion, but, rather, to tether it to his repudiation of perfectionism: If one would do the least damage (stop "people from devouring one another like fish"), then one must be aware of the always-lurking possibility of widespread disintegration, the unraveling of social peace, and the spread of devastating fear. If one brings the city of God into too tight a relationship to the city of man, then the latter begins to make claims that take on the character of the ultimate. At the same time, because the earthly city gestures toward the ultimate, any within its ranks that threaten to implode it and that seek their own form of power by putting other souls in harm's way fall under the sway of episcopal correction.[22] Given the routine use of overt coercive techniques in late antiquity, what seems most interesting is how much Augustine repudiated, and troubled himself over, not how much he retained.

Most importantly, the Augustinian is always a radical *in situ*. Here Dietrich Bonhoeffer's move from "good Lutheran" to martyred anti-Nazi resister is instructive, for Bonhoeffer's slow emergence as a powerful opponent of the Nazified German state is based on solid Augustinian principles concerning the limits to what earthly dominion can rightfully be about. When it trangresses those limits, it must be called to account, placed under harsh judgment. We would not even be able to mount such efforts if we were wholly and entirely con-formers; if our lives were lived solely on a horizontal plane. What the *civitas dei* offers is a reference point that is also, potentially, a resistance point. Most of the time, presumably and hopefully, one need not move into the harsh severing of those ties that bind us to the earthly city. But sometimes it is necessary. Yet it would not even be possible—this form of revolt—if we could not get outside of conventional arrangements, rhetoric, terms of approval and disapproval and the like. The Christian should be a disturber of the peace, or, in the words of Pope John Paul II, a "sign of contradiction." Christian hope does not permit "a politically sterile withdrawal," in Markus's words.[23]

Milbank, in part in response to Markus's take on things, puts a somewhat different spin on what Augustine has accomplished and deeded to us with the allegory of the two cities. Milbank emphasizes the social dimension of the life of the saints, insisting that Augustine criticized the Roman order in part because it promoted self-love and hence self-isolation. The Church, then, is set up "in opposition to" one notion of the city. But it is also in itself a 'political' (Milbank uses the scare quotes) reality of a sort. That is, it is a community with a notion of transformed citizenship. This community works to overcome the classical antinomy between *oikos* and *polis* "because Augustine allows both household and city to stand, yet conceives a kind of micro-macrocosmic relationship between the two."[24] In the world as we found it and know it, there will be many cities, just as there are many households in a city. Or we can at least hope this is the case, for if it were not, it would signify that we had moved into the desert of a worldwide *imperium*, with its homogenizing urges, analogous to that of the Roman *Pax*.

Milbank would suggest to Markus that care of body and soul always involve discipline and sometimes involve coercion or, certainly, *authoritative determinations*. But "the goal of *ecclesia*, the city of

God, is not collective glory, as if the city were itself a hero, any more than it is the production of heroic individuals."[25] This *ecclesia* is not 'church' in our modern understanding, as an institution standing over against that equally abstract entity, 'state,' but, rather, one of the multiple forms of mediation between individuals and the world—with this difference: *ecclesia* recognizes a singular Mediator, as other institutions do not, and it is through analogy with Christ's Mediation between God and the human person that the church's relation of believer to the world can, in part, be understood. Milbank sums this up—this new set of ideas about human earthly possibility—with a list of points numbered 1 through 4, which I will here repeat:

1. micro/macro cosmic isomorphism;
2. the non-subordination of either part to whole or whole to part;
3. the presence of the whole in every part; and
4. positioning within an indefinite shifting sequence rather than a fixed totality.[26]

For Milbank, where Augustine begins to slip in the matter of coercion is not so much a story of a fall from some pristine and noninstitutionalized Christian moment, but inheres in Augustine's discussion of the way in which the Church, having denied "ontological necessity to sovereign rule and absolute ownership," must nevertheless cooperate with, live among and within, and even use such rule in its earthly pilgrimage. Over the long term, only "non-coercive persuasion" works to attain peace "because the free consent of will is necessary to this goal."[27] But earthly rule is always a tragic rule—necessarily so—involving the disciplining of sin; thus *potestas* and *auctoritas* are twins. But the problem, within Augustine's framework, is just this: because he sees in absolute rule, or absolute anything on this earth, certain sins—the triumph of a mistaken notion of self—then punishment, even if the aim is instruction and reproof, must itself "inflict some harm, however temporary"; hence, such punishment "has an inherently negative, private relationship to Being, and cannot therefore, by Augustine's own lights, escape the taint of sin."[28]

Small wonder Augustine clings to the insistence that *all* punishment, for whatever reason, is a tragic risk "and that Christianity should seek to reduce the sphere of its operation."[29] If anything, Augustine's recognition, deep down, is more mordant than I here allow, acknowledging, as he does, that *any* exercise of power that involves imposition tends to feed violence. Violence, in turn, threatens to destroy or undermine Augustine's two basic principles: do no harm and love God and your neighbor. Striking this note is important—one does not want to evade Augustine's approval of coercive measures (as a final resort, not a first strike), against those he saw as an internal threat to *mater ecclesia*. But the political *gravamen* seems to me to lie elsewhere, and it is to this I next turn.

The One and the Many Reconfigured

Hannah Arendt loved one particular Augustine quotation. She used it over and over again: *Initium ut esset homo creatus est*—"that a beginning be made man was created."[30] Indeed, Arendt's understanding of, and emphasis on, human plurality—on the distance between people; her concern about human reduction to conforming isolates—all this is deeply Augustinian. As with everything else about antique thought, Augustine shifts the terms of discourse away from *the one* and *the many* as usually understood, into something that is best cast along rather different lines. If the motto on all legal United States tender is "out of many, one," Augustine offers an alternative: "out of one, many." That a beginning was made, man was created—one singular human being. This is very important.

God did not begin with the human species but with singularity. With other creatures, whether those of solitary habit "who

walk alone and love solitude," or those who are "gregarious, pre-
ferring to live in flocks and herds," he "commanded many to
come into existence at once."[31] But not so the human person.
Here God created "one individual; but that did not mean that he
was to remain alone, bereft of human society. God's intention
was that in this way the unity of human society and the bonds of
human sympathy be more emphatically brought home to man,
if men were bound together not merely by likeness in nature but
also by the feeling of kinship."[32] Woman is brought into being
from a portion of the first single human being and from this the
human race gets its start. What's important about this starting
point? Augustine explains as we move to Book XIV. Augustine re-
iterates God's purpose—that "the human race should not merely
be united in a society by natural likeness but should also be
bound together by the 'bond of peace.'"[33] Spread out upon the
face of the earth, living under many customs and distinguished
by a "complex variety of languages, arms, and dress," all partici-
pate in that fellowship we call human society; all are marked by
the point of origin from one; all are called to membership in the
two cities. One of the first laws that emerged was the law of marriage, a tie that binds and that, in turn, makes possible wider affections: the filaments of affection must not stop at the portal to
the *domus*.

Indeed, we learn about neighborliness and reciprocity from
this first beginning, for this is how we all began following the
creation of the first human being. "The aim was that one man
should not combine many relationships in his one self, but that
those connections should be separated and spread among individuals, and that in this way they should help to bind social life
more effectively by involving in their plurality a plurality of persons. 'Father' and 'father-in-law', for instance, are names denot-
ing two different relationships. Thus affection stretches over a
greater number when each person has one man for father and
another for father-in-law."[34] Augustine goes on to discourse
about mothers-in-law and sisters-in-law and and cousins and

grandchildren and the spouses of all of these and pretty soon you have a wide social network.

The social tie is "not confined to a small group" but extends "more widely to a large number with the multiplying links of kinship."[35] With this extension in kinship comes prohibitions. Marriage between cousins is one Augustine cites. And he explains:

> Yet no one doubts that the modern prohibition of marriage between cousins is an advance in civilized standards. And this not only because of the point I have already made, namely, that the ties of kinship are thereby multiplied, in that one person cannot stand in a double relationship, when this can be divided between two persons, and so the scope of kinship may be enlarged. There is another reason. There is in human conscience a certain mysterious and inherent sense of decency, this is natural and also admirable, which ensures that if kinship gives a woman a claim to honour and respect, she is shielded from the lust (and lust it is, although it results in procreation) which, as we know, brings blushes even to the chastity of marriage.[36]

Any society that loses this sense of decency, with its concomitant sense of shame, is a society in very big trouble indeed, Augustine would argue.

The importance of plurality, of the many emerging from a unique one, cannot be underestimated in Augustine's work. From *one* creates a fragile but real ontology of peace, or relative peacefulness. Bonds of affection tied human beings from the start. Bonds of kinship and affection bound them further. The more these relationships are dispersed, finally encompassing the entire globe, and in light of the confusion and confounding of human languages, the more difficult it is to repair to this fundamental kinship or sociality in order to strike a blow for peace and against war. Yet that's when it becomes especially important. This is no bland assertion that we are all alike. Augustine knows better. We are very far apart indeed. Remember, it is easier to have fellowship with one's dog than with someone speaking a foreign tongue. Nevertheless, there is something like a common nature and it is this thread of commonality that supports both individuality and plurality; that helps to constitute us as individuals; that helps to preserve the space between us—out of one, many ones, each a new beginning; yet these many ones share a nature in common.

> [C]ould anyone fail to see, on rational consideration, how marvellous it is that, despite the countless numbers of mankind, and despite the great similarity among men through their possession of a common nature, each individual has his own unique individual appearance? The truth is that if there were not this underlying similarity man could not be distinguished as a separate species from the other animals, while at the same time, without those individual differences, one man could not be distinguished from another. Thus we acknowledge that men are alike, and equally we discover that they are different. Now it is the observation of the differences between men that should arouse our wonder; for the likeness would seem to be normal, as something demanded by our common nature. And yet because it is rarities that rouse wonder, we are much more astonished when we find two people so alike that we are always, or very frequently, making mistakes when we try to distinguish them.[37]

This is a preachment of such good sense, especially in the light of the passions of our own moment when we are enjoined to homogenize difference on the basis of racial, gender, or ethnic criteria, yet, at the same time, urged to strenuously resist commonality with any who embody some other principle of group difference, that one would like to enshrine it, laminate it, place it on every media mogul's and opinion maker's desk. But one knows better. For the time being we seem to have lost the *via media* between denying differences or absolutizing them definitively; between presuming a too thoroughgoing unanimity and negating the possibility of any commonality. This is but one of the many reasons we, as a society, are in trouble.

Peace and War: Why Augustine Still Matters

The *saeculum* is the here and now.[38] It is in the here and now that war and peace get played out. If the Christian is a disturber of a false peace, he or she yearns for a more authentic representation of earthly peace as that which partakes in the *pax aeterna*. One can hope for what is possible to obtain. An imperfect but nonetheless real earthly peace lies within the realm of the possible. Peter Brown notes that, for Augustine, *saeculum* is "all-embracing and inescapable." The Christian caught in temporality is pressed by "the selfsame press as the bad." The press is Augustine's analogy to an olive press, squeezing olives for oil. Thus we are pressed. But our life of fellowship—a *vita socialis sanctorum*—calls us, not to perfection, but to relative peace.[39] The Heavenly City is a perfect vision of peace. But there is earthly work to be done in the name of peace.

Augustine's complex discourse on peace begins with his devastating send-up of the pretensions of the Roman Empire. He anticipates modern critical strategies when he strips "off the deceptive veils," removes "the whitewash of illusion," and subjects "the facts to a strict inspection." Take away the screens of "the splendid titles of 'honour' and 'victory'"—really "senseless notions"—and what one finds are "crimes . . . great evils to vex and exhaust the whole human race." Rome was conquered by her own lust to dominate as she triumphed over others: "Think of all the battles fought, all the blood poured out, so that almost all the nations of Italy, by whose help the Roman Empire wielded that overwhelming power, should be subjugated as if they were barbarous savages."[40] The only law for Roman conquerors was that of vengeance—even when peace and victory were proclaimed.

"Peace and War had a competition in cruelty; and Peace won the prize." Augustine shifts to biting irony where the follies and fancies of Rome are concerned: "For the men whom War cut down were bearing arms; Peace slaughtered the defenceless." Let us not be taken in by "empty bombast" that blunts "the edge of our critical faculties . . . by high-sounding words like 'peoples,' 'realms,' 'provinces.'" A kingdom without justice (most kingdoms most of the time) is a criminal gang on a large scale. Augustine repeats the story of the rejoinder given by a captured pirate to Alexander the Great when Alexander queried him about his idea in infesting the sea. "And the pirate answered, with uninhibited insolence, 'The same as yours, in infesting the earth! But because I do it with a tiny craft, I'm called a pirate: because you have a mighty navy, you're called an emperor.'"[41]

The Romans, Augustine suggests, should have erected a monument to a goddess named "Aliena"—foreign injustice—because they had made such good use of her. What does he mean? He means that the Romans proclaimed all their wars defensive; it was, therefore, necessary to conjure up an implacable foreign foe in order to justify these ravages—behold Aliena, the foreign threat. Rome's *imperium* cannot be justified, even on Augustine's nonperfectionist standard, because it promotes an unjust idea of "ownership which allows the owner to 'do as he likes' with what he owns," including *plebs* and foreign hostages and peoples.[42] For Rome, peace is just another name for *dominium*. Think, Augustine tells us, of the cost of "this achievement" of the Roman Pax. "Consider the scale of those wars, with all that slaughter of human beings, all the human blood that was shed!" If you reflect on this, you will wage only limited, justifiable wars even as you lament the fact that they sometimes must be waged given "the injustice of the opposing side." I will get to just, or justifiable war, in a moment. Let's linger a bit longer on the other side, the realm of war as the expression of *libido dominandi*.

Milbank argues that, according to Augustine, the Romans thought that there could be virtue only "where there is something to be defeated. . . ." Thus, the story "Rome tells about its own foundations" is a story of a murder of one brother by another who

> is also the enslaver of *clienteles* to whom he offered protection against foreign enemies. In battle, Romulus invoked the staying hand of Jupiter, who then received the title Ustator. The supreme God, therefore, like the founding hero, arises merely as the limiter of a preceding disorder. . . . Mythical beginnings of legal order are therefore traced back to the arbitrary limitation of violence by violence. . . . And, according to Augustine, the Romans continued to 'live out' the *mythos:* within the city gates the goddess most celebrated was *Bellona,* the virtues most crowned with glory were the military ones.[43]

This point is seconded by Rowan Williams, who reminds us that Augustine observes, as early as Book I, *The City of God,* that Carthage played a rather major role in "securing order and justice in Rome. The destruction of the Republic's great rival meant that the *libido dominandi* hitherto checked by the need for discipline and unity, and to some extent exercised in defense against an external aggressor, came to be exercised within the state, producing gross inequality and injustice. Aggression not dealt with in the inner ecology of social beings seeks outlets—if not against a stranger, then by making strangers of fellow-citizens."[44] Is this not what we are up to in American society? Are we not busy building barriers between ourselves, bustling away, proclaiming that we cannot speak to one another, cannot understand one another, and must not have anything to do with one another?[45]

There are, as I already noted, occasional real wars of defense. The wise ruler is no aggressor and takes up arms only with great reluctance and penitence. (Remember, no state is an absolute value, so no state can be defended absolutely through means that are, simply, unacceptable.) Here Augustine joins the ranks of just war thinkers; thus, even as he is frequently lodged as a forebear of political realism, he is similarly credited as the great-great-grandfather of just war. There is no reason he cannot be both, of course. That turns on what we understand by realism and by just war. Now Augustine does appreciate what modern international relations thinkers call the *security dilemma*. People never possess a kingdom "so securely as not to fear subjugation by their enemies; in fact, such is the instability of human affairs that no people has ever been allowed such a degree of tranquillity as to remove all dread of hostile attacks on their life in this world. That place, then, which is promised as a dwelling of such peace and security is eternal, and is reserved for eternal beings, in 'the mother, the Jerusalem which is free'."[46] One must simply live with this shadow, a penumbra of fear and worry on this earth. But one must not give oneself over to it, not without overweening justification.

When one capitulates to this fear, one gets Empire and this, in turn, has

> given rise to wars of a worse kind, namely, social and civic wars, by which mankind is more lamentably disquieted either when fighting is going on in the hope of bringing hostilities eventually to a peaceful end, or when there are fears that hostilities will break out again. If I were to try to describe, with an eloquence worthy of the subject, the many and multifarious disasters, the dour and dire necessities, I could not possibly be adequate to the theme and there would be no end to this protracted discussion. But the wise man, they say, will wage just wars. Surely, if he remembers that he is a human being, he will rather lament the fact that he is faced with the necessity of waging just wars; for if they were not just, he would not have to engage in them, and consequently there would be no wars for a wise man.

The just ruler waging a justifiable war of necessity to rescue the innocent from certain destruction, for example, doesn't look down the road and see parades and banners and kudos all round, but sees mangled bodies and destroyed villages and torn and shredded human lives: he acknowledges "the misery of them."[47] Augustine's grudging endorsement of the lesser evil enters his discourse at this point. But the end game is not talk of power, or sovereignty, or national interest, but only of peace. From the tigress purring over her cubs, to human fellowship in all its forms, peace, even a pale peace unworthy of the name, is the ultimate aim of conflict. This is worth belaboring. Here my reference point is Book XIX, chapter 12, "Peace is the instinctive aim of all creatures, and is even the ultimate purpose of war." Oddly enough, when people fight it is to draw fighting to a close. From robber bands to rulers, each maintains "some kind of shadow of peace, at least with those whom he cannot kill. . . ." Each is anxious to be at peace in his own home. There is a lingering sweetness here, tethered to a dangerous temptation. For if the robber band leader who wants peace in his own home construes that peace as having his "wife and children" at "his beck and call" and who, when they do not respond immediately, "scolds and punishes," if such a one were then offered "the servitude of a larger number, of a city, maybe, or a whole nation, on the condition that they should all show the same subservience he had demanded from his household, then he would no longer lurk like a brigand in his hide-out; he would raise himself on high as a king for all to see—although the same greed and malignity would persist in him."[48]

The desire to be *at peace* is too often a desire to *impose one's will*, to subject others. This leads to pridefulness, a "perverted imitation of God." And pridefulness, in turn, spurs more temptation to vanquish. Disorder becomes the means to order, the order of body, mind, and fellowship we all, in some way, desire. But disorder feeds on itself and we undermine the very preconditions for that which alone would help to satisfy us this side of the eschaton. No one should be mistaken about the lust to dominate that is so hopelessly intermingled with the yearning for peace. That is why we must be ever vigilant about the yearning for peace and whether what we seek is the quiet of destruction: *Carthago delenda est* as the solution to our woes.

Consider, then, Augustine's story of poor, bereft Cacus, a monster. He holds up this story as a parable for all in the *saeculum*.

Let us, however, suppose such a man as is described in the verse of epic legends, a creature so unsociable and savage that they perhaps preferred to call him a semi-human rather than a human being. Now although his kingdom was the solitude of a dreadful cavern, and although he was so unequalled in wickedness that a name was found for him derived from that quality (he was called Cacus, and *kakos* is the Greek word for 'wicked'); although he had no wife with whom to exchange endearments, no children to play with when little or to give orders to when they were a little bigger, no friends with whom to enjoy a chat, not even his father, Vulcan (he was happier than his father only in this important respect—that he did not beget another such monster as himself); although he never gave anything to anyone, but took what he wanted from anyone he could and removed, when he could, anyone he wished to remove; despite all this, in the very solitude of his cave, the floor of which, in the poet's description

> reeked ever with the blood of recent slaughter

his only desire was for a peace in which no one should disturb him, and no man's violence, or the dread of it, should trouble his repose. Above all, he desired to be at peace with his own body; and in so far as he achieved this, all was well with them. He gave orders and his limbs obeyed. But his mortal nature rebelled against him because of its insatiable desires, and stirred up the civil strife of hunger, intending to dissociate the soul from the body and to exclude it; and then he sought with all possible haste to pacify that mortal nature, and to that end he ravished, murdered, and devoured. And thus, for all his monstrous savagery, his aim was still to ensure peace, for the preservation of his life, by these monstrous and savage methods.[49]

Behold poor Cacus! We know him well. That is Augustine's solemn warning to all of us.

As with all other received categories in our time, Augustine does not sit easily within either the realist or the just-war camps.

He makes war much harder to justify than many just-war thinkers do, and certainly he is as concerned by what gets stirred up even among just warriors as he is by the depredations done to one's foes. No one walks away from a justifiable defensive war or war of rescue unscathed. With modern realists he shares a deep skepticism. Michael Loriaux has argued that, in fact, Augustine offers a much richer psychology than the highly simplified, highly stylized psychology of current academic realism with its very thin view of human beings and human motivation.[50] Loriaux urges modern realists to return to Augustine, to take a refresher course, as it were, in humankind's "self-inflicted alienation" and temptation for coercion and empire. "Augustine," he writes, "is as skeptical about our capacity to define a national interest and to distinguish between expedient and rash action as he is about the prospects of achieving the *teleiosis* in the *saeculum*. He invites us to acknowledge the vagaries of the human will as it intercedes between rationality and action."[51]

Now is the time to get sober and to remember what St. Augustine taught: war and strife, however just the cause, stir up temptations to ravish and to devour, often in order to ensure peace. Just war is and must remain a cautionary tale of domestic and international order, a story of the requirements and purposeful uses of power and order, a lens through which to look at the heart of what constitutes what is called peace. The earthly city is never free from the dangers of bloodshed, sedition, and war. A human being cannot even be certain of "his own conduct on the morrow," let alone specify and adjudicate that of others in ways he or she foreordains. In this world of discontinuities and profound yearnings, of sometimes terrible necessities, a human being can yet strive to maintain or to create an order that approximates justice, to prevent the worst from happening, and to resist the seductive lure of imperial grandiosity.

Augustine invites us to do this and more. The last words shall be his:

For peace is so great a good that even in relation to the affairs of earth and of our mortal state no word ever falls more gratefully upon the ear, nothing is desired with greater longing, in fact, nothing better can be found. So if I decide to discourse about it at somewhat greater length, I shall not, I think, impose a burden on my readers, not only because I shall be speaking of the end of the City which is the subject of this work, but also because of the delightfulness of peace, which is dear to the heart of all mankind.[52]

Loving Crazy Horse and Augustine

I am loathe to close, knowing I have just scratched the surface, moved trippingly over but a few of the keys, in exploring the work—and that with but a few themes in mind—of this extraordinary figure. One feels rather like Salieri stunned by Mozart—with this difference, at least in my case. Rather than resentment and ire, when I find myself confronted with the monumental nature of Augustine's works, I am extraordinarily grateful. Like that world Augustine so loved, his work beckons to us and bids us explore, contest, come-to-grips, sit and visit for a spell or, of course, walk away. Thus, in bidding him adieu for now, I am acknowledging that I, for one, will return to him over and over again. He is, after all, a companion on the footpath. There is so much that hasn't been touched. Let me introduce one final theme, briefly, before I take my leave.

I concluded chapter 5 by alerting us to Augustine's warnings that any war stirs up a desire to ravish, even if we manage somehow to resist the temptation. War, one might suggest, is an arena for the unchaining of *libido dominandi*. Ideally, peace should be the "object of your choice" and war, even if a necessity, should not be willed.[1] A tall order and Augustine knows it. Better, by far, that war as an occasion for willing, and (hopefully) at least partial nilling, not arise. As well, in chastizing others in secular or churchly arenas, one should avoid, if one can, "harshness . . . or . . . severity, or . . . overbearing methods."[2] Persuasion rather than intimidation, if at all possible.

There is a further issue this gestures toward—Augustine's repudiation of a teleology of violence, whether as means or end.
The attraction of violence is great. In her essay *OnViolence*, Hannah
Arendt asks what historic transformations and discursive practices made possible an unsettling consensus "among political
theorists from Left to Right . . . that violence is nothing more
than the most flagrant manifestation of power."[3] Her answer is
multiple. Although she indicts features of several traditions
(among others, notions of absolute sovereignty; command-
obedience conceptions of law; the intrusion of biologism into
political thought), she is especially biting in her judgment of
Marxism and all Marxian modes on this score. Its "great trust in
the dialectical 'power of negation,'" Arendt argues, either soothes
its adherents, or mobilizes them, into believing that evil is "but a
temporary manifestation of a still-hidden good."[4] She laments
the move to the glorification of violence in the student movement in the United States by the late 1960s and early 1970s. She
lambastes Sartre, who proclaimed that violence "'like Achilles'
lance, can heal the wounds it has inflicted.' If this were true,"
Arendt continues scathingly, "revenge would be the cure-all for
most of our ills."[5]

As I have already argued, Augustine offers not merely a condemnation of this appetite for unbridled *cupiditas* in the form of
the *libido dominandi*, he gives us the great gift of an alternative way
of thinking and being in the world, a way that is in many vital respects available to those who are not doctrinally Augustine's
brothers and sisters. In the twentieth century, justification and
rationalization of violence as the *modus operandi* of social change
introduces an element of remorseless moral absolutism into politics. The delectation of mounds of bodies stacked up as our
handiwork, the riveting possibility of salutary bloodletting, grips
the imagination. The result is a pile of garbage and a pile of bodies. The fact of death becomes the primary political statement.
Inflamed militants march to the Grim Reaper's habituating

drumbeat. The cadence is nigh irresistible to many. Augustine would have us resist—in the name of love.

The search for what Albert Camus called "the dialectical miracle" is a decision to call total servitude 'freedom.' "But," as Camus writes in his own lucid and exemplary work *The Rebel*, much understudied and underestimated, having itself been caught up in the dogmatic Sartrian-Marxist buzz saw and dismissed by the literati proclaiming their own revolutionary rectitude and virtue, "total freedom is no more easy to conquer than individual freedom. To ensure man's empire over the world, it is necessary to suppress in the world and in man everything that escapes the Empire, everything that does not come under the reign of quantity: and this is an endless undertaking."[6] Camus's is an Augustinian take on a lust for empire that cannot cease until it has flattened everything in sight and made it its own. It is the peace of conquest. There is another vision of peace, "so dear to the hearts" of humankind, as we have already seen.

But enough. A few years ago I read a wonderful book called *The Great Plains* by Ian Frazier. Because I hail from the West and know something of the sparse grandeur of the Great Plains, I was much taken with this work. I found especially powerful Frazier's elegy for the great chief Crazy Horse, regarded by Indian and non-Indian alike, Frazier tells us, "with a reverence which borders on the holy." Of course, there are many who do not get it, this love of Crazy Horse, just as there are many whose hearts do not unlock when they read *The Confessions*. But Frazier? Well, he loves Crazy Horse and he tells us why.

> Personally, I love Crazy Horse because even the most basic outline of his life shows how great he was; because he remained himself from the moment of his birth to the moment he died; because he knew exactly where he wanted to live, and never left; because he may have surrendered, but he was never defeated in battle; because, although he was killed, even the Army admitted he was never captured; because he was so free that he didn't know what a jail

looked like; because at the most desperate moment of his life he only cut Little Big Man on the hand; because, unlike many people all over the world, when he met white men he was not diminished by the encounter; because his dislike of the oncoming civilization was prophetic; because the idea of becoming a farmer apparently never crossed his mind; because he didn't end up in the Dry Tortugas; because he never met the President; because he never rode on a train, slept in a boardinghouse, ate at a table; because he never wore a medal or a top hat or any other thing that white men gave him; because he made sure that his wife was safe before going to where he expected to die; because although Indian agents, among themselves, sometimes referred to Red Cloud as "Red" and Spotted Tail as "Spot," they never used a diminutive of him; because, deprived of freedom, power, occupation, culture, trapped in a situation where bravery was invisible, he was still brave; because he fought in self-defense, and took no one with him when he died; because, like the rings of Saturn, the carbon atom, and the underwater reef, he belonged to a category of phenomena which our technology had not then advanced far enough to photograph; because no photograph or painting or even sketch of him exists; because he is not the Indian on the nickel, the tobacco pouch, or the apple crate. . . . Mortally wounded, frothing at the mouth, grinding his teeth in pain, he chose the floor instead. What a distance there is between that cot and the floor! On the cot, he would have been, in some sense, "ours": an object of pity, an accident victim, "the noble red man, the last of his race, etc., etc." But on the floor Crazy Horse was Crazy Horse still. . . . On the floor, he said goodbye to his father and Touch the Clouds, the last of the thousands that once followed him. And on the floor, still as far from white men as the limitless continent they once dreamed of, he died. . . . Lying where he chose, Crazy Horse showed the rest of us where we are standing.[7]

He showed the rest of us where we are standing: thus it is with Augustine of Hippo. The image of the old man in his study, rereading his works, going over them another time, commenting on them, knowing it may all be ashes and dust soon enough, it may all disappear—*The Confessions, The City of God*, the lot—he perseveres. He meets with his brothers in monastic life; greets his brothers and sisters in *mater ecclesia*; does battle with his foes; prays to his God. And he remains deeply—to his own mind, at times, even dangerously—in love with the world. So I love Augustine because he could write like this about flowers and leaves:

> All those castaways, so to speak, doomed to perish so swiftly, could not . . . display such perfection of graceful harmony in their shapes, were it not that they received their form from the eternal abode of the intelligible and changeless 'form' which contains them all together in itself. This is what the Lord Jesus tells us in the passage where he says,
>
> Consider the lilies of the field: they do not work, or spin. Yet I tell you, Solomon in all his splendour was not clothed like one of these. . . .[8]

Because he marveled over oddities and rarities:

> Some people can even move their ears, either one at a time or both together. Others without moving the head can bring the whole scalp—all the part covered with hair—down towards the forehead and bring it back again at will. Some can swallow an incredible number of various articles and then with a slight contraction of the diaphragm, can produce, as if out of a bag, any article they please, in perfect condition. There are others who imitate the cries of birds and beasts and the voices of any other men, reproducing them so accurately as to be quite indistinguishable from the originals, unless they are seen. A number of people produce at will such musical sounds from their behind (without any stink) that they seem to be singing from that region. I know from my own experience of a man who used to sweat whenever he chose; and it is a well-known fact that some people can weep at will and shed floods of tears.[9]

Because he experienced astonished childlike awe in the presence of even the humblest natural phenomena:

Let us consider the marvels of lime. Apart from the fact that it grows white by the action of fire which makes other things dirty . . . , it also in some most mysterious way takes fire into itself from the fire, and it stores the fire inside the mass of lime, which is cold to the touch, so secretly that it does not present itself to our senses in any way at all but, when it has been discovered by experiment, it is known to be asleep within the mass even when there is no evidence of its presence. That is why we call it 'quicklime', living lime, as if the fire hidden within it were the invisible soul of a visible body. But the really wonderful thing is that when it is quenched, it is kindled! For to get rid of its hidden fire, water is poured on it, or it is plunged into water, and then it grows hot, though it was cold before; and that is the effect of water, which cools other substances when they are hot. And so, as that lump of lime expires, so to speak, the fire hidden in it makes its appearance at its departure; and thereafter the lime is so cold in death, as it were, that if water is applied to it it will not blaze up, and what was called 'quicklime' is now called 'quenched' or 'killed' lime. Could anything be added to make this marvel more astounding? Yes, there is something more. If you use oil, instead of water, the lime does not grow hot, whether oil is poured on the lime or the lime is plunged in the oil! And yet oil is fuel of fire, and water is not![10]

The world, for Augustine, was a "compressed pile of blessings." He must now be counted among its wonders, he who could end that most extraordinary of books with these words:

And now, as I think, I have discharged my debt, with the completion, by God's help, of his huge work. It may be too much for some, too little for others. Of both these groups I ask forgiveness. But of those for whom it is enough I make this request: that they do not thank me, but join with me in rendering thanks to God. Amen. Amen.[11]

This man who desired "not only a devout reader, but also an open-minded critic," gets too few of each, or both, in our harsh and cynical time.[12] But he perdures.

NOTES

1. Why Augustine? Why Now?

1. Johan Huizinga, *The Waning of the Middle Ages* (Garden City, N.Y.: Doubleday Anchor Books, 1954.)

2. Hannah Arendt, *Between Past and Future* (New York: Penguin Books, 1968), pp. 3–16.

3. P. R. L. Brown, "Political Society," in Richard Markus, ed., *Augustine: A Collection of Critical Essays* (Garden City, N.Y.: Doubleday Anchor Books, 1972), p. 311.

4. St. Augustine, Letter 138, *The Letters of St. Augustine*, Fathers of the Church series, 20 (Washington, D.C.: Catholic University of America Press, 1953), p. 47.

5. Augustine, *The City of God* (Baltimore: Penguin, 1985), Book XXII, chapter 24, pp. 1072–73.

6. Ibid., Book XIX, chapter 12, p. 868.

7. Augustine, *The Confessions* (New York: Penguin Books, 1961), Book IV, p. 76.

8. Peter Brown, *Augustine of Hippo* (Berkeley: University of California Press, 1967), p. 181.

9. Augustine, *The Confessions*, Book X, pp. 211–12.

10. Charles Norris Cochrane, *Christianity and Classical Culture* (New York: Galaxy Book, 1959), p. 378.

11. Ibid., p. 379.

12. Paul Rigby, "Paul Ricoeur, Freudianism, and Augustine's *Confessions*," *Journal of the American Academy of Religion* 53, no. 1, (March 1985), 93. It should be added that Freud would be appalled at many of the attempts to instantly diagnose Augustine. If one reads his essays on

Leonardo da Vinci or Dostoevsky, one sees a subtle mind at work, whatever one thinks of the attempt. But Freud at least allows that the great works stand on their own.

13. Ibid., p. 95.

14. *The Confessions*, Book IX, p. 199.

15. Ibid., Book IX, pp. 204–5.

16. Donald Capps, "Augustine as Narcissist: Comments on Paul Rigby's 'Paul Ricoeur, Freudianism, and Augustine's *Confessions*,'" *Journal of the American Academy of Religion* 53, no. 1 (March 1985), 116.

17. Ibid., p. 117.

18. See Coles's fascinating discussion in *Self/Power/Other: Political Theory and Dialogical Ethics* (Cornell: Cornell University Press, 1992).

19. *The Confessions*, Book III, p. 60.

20. Ibid., p. 154.

21. Ibid., Book I, p. 39.

22. Ibid.

23. Ibid., Book I, p.28.

24. Ibid., Book III, p. 60.

25. Brown, *Augustine of Hippo*, p. 429.

26. Augustine, *The Retractions* (Washington, D.C.: Catholic University of America, 1968), p. 130. "At least, as far as I am concerned, they had this effect on me while I was writing them and they continue to have it when I am reading them." I have used the Peter Brown translation of this sentence in the text. (See his *Augustine of Hippo*, p. 165.)

27. See John Milbank, *Theology and Social Theory* (London: Basil Blackwell, 1990), p. 401. I earlier made similar points in my discussion of Augustine in both *Public Man, Private Woman* (Princeton: Princeton University Press, 2nd ed., 1993) and in *Women and War* (New York: Basic Books, 1987).

28. A task not unlike cleaning out the Aegean stable—it can't really be done but it must be tried.

29. Augustine of Hippo, *Selected Writings* (New York: Paulist Press, 1984), Homilies on the Psalms, Psalm 121, p. 238.

30. Václav Havel, "Forgetting That We Are Not God," *First Things*, March 1995, pp. 49–50.

31. Peter Brown, *Augustine of Hippo*, p. 156.

2. The Earthly City and Its Discontents

1. Augustine, *The City of God*, ed. David Knowles (Baltimore: Penguin Books, 1972), p. 5. Hereafter references will be abbreviated DCD.

2. I was playing a bit fast and loose with "analytic" here it seems, not really thinking about the debate over positivism.

3. George Armstrong Kelly, *Politics and Religious Consciousness in America* (New Brunswick, N.J.: Transaction, 1984), p. 175.

4. See John Neville Figgis's fiddling around with the terms in *The Political Aspects of S. Augustine's City of God* (Gloucester, Mass.: Peter Smith, 1963).

5. P. L. B. Brown, "Political Society," in Robert A. Markus, ed., *Augustine: A Collection of Critical Essays* (Garden City, N.Y.: Doubleday Anchor Books, 1972), p. 312.

6. Kelly, *Politics and Religious Consciousness*, p. 261.

7. Jean Bethke Elshtain, *Public Man, Private Woman: Women in Social and Political Thought* (Princeton: Princeton University Press, 1981), p. 64.

8. Augustine, DCD, Book XIX, chapter 6, p. 860.

9. Ibid., chapter 5, p. 858.

10. Ibid., p. 859.

11. Ibid., chapter 7, p. 861.

12. On this see Peter Brown's wonderful book *The Cult of the Saints* (Chicago: University of Chicago Press, 1981).

13. Augustine, DCD, Book IX, chapter 5, p. 350.

14. Ibid., Book X, chapter 1, p. 375.

15. Ibid., Book XI, chapter 8, p. 437.

16. Ibid., Book XI, chapter 26, p. 459.

17. Ibid., Book XIII, chapter 11, p. 520.

18. *The Confessions*, Book I, pp. 25–26.

19. Ibid., Book V, p. 97.

20. Ibid., p. 108.

21. This is a rough summation of Book X, pp. 211–12.

22. Ibid., Book XI, p. 256.

23. Ibid., this is actually from Book XII, p. 289.

24. Ibid., p. 296.

25. Ibid., p. 303.

26. Ibid., Book XIII, p. 335.

27. DCD, Book XIX, chapter 16, p. 876.

28. Although this theme is taken up by John Milbank in *Theology and Social Theory* (London: Basil Blackwell, 1990), I here rely on my argument from *Public Man, Private Woman*. Although Milbank appears unfamiliar with my 1981 work, I offer an interpretation that prefigures his own.

29. Rowman Williams, "Politics and the Soul: A Reading of *The City of God*," *Milltown Studies* 19, no. 20 (1987): 58.

30. DCD, Book XI, chapter 1, p. 429.

31. Ibid., Book XIX, chapter 12, p. 866.

32. Ibid., Book XXII, chapter 22, p. 1065.

33. Ibid., Book XIX, chapter 3, p. 851.

34. Ibid., chapter 8, p. 862. Augustine's target here, of course, is Stoicism.

35. Ibid., chapter 16, p. 876.

36. Augustine, *Select Letters*, trans. J. H. Baxter (Cambridge, Mass.: Harvard University Press, 1993), no. 24 (Ep. XCI), p. 155.

37. John Milbank, *Theology and Social Theory*, pp. 390–91.

38. Both Milbank and I make this point. My discussion is in *Women and War*.

39. Brown, *Augustine of Hippo*, p. 324.

40. *The Confessions*, Book XIII, p. 344. Augustine goes on to suggest, rather vaguely, that in "sex she is physically subject to him in the same way as our natural impulses need to be subjected to the reasoning power of the mind. . . ." But this is underargued and clearly not a central point. Here the analogy breaks down. For if woman is absolutely equal to man in nature and intelligence, the grounds for his relative authority over hers, in the interest of felicity, cannot be analogous to the mind in relation to the impulses. This is what might be called a "throwaway" line, and Augustine's account of creation itself undermines it.

41. Augustine, DCD, Book XVI, chapter 8, pp. 662–63.

42. Ibid., Book XIV, chapter 14, p. 574.

43. Augustine, *The Trinity* (Washington, D.C.: Catholic University of America Press, 1992), Book Twelve, chapter 7, pp. 351–52.

44. Ibid., p. 354; chapter 8, p. 355.

45. Ibid., chapter 11, p. 361.

46. *Select Letters*, no. 60, p. 503.

47. Ibid., no. 11, pp. 93–95.

48. DCD, Book I, chapter 19, p. 28. It is important to be clear about all this. Some have suggested that Augustine's emphasis on not having sinned in that no "willing" was there, is anemic and still leaves the woman open to "external" charges of culpability. But this radically interiorizes Augustine's discussion. Remember, he is systematically dismantling the codes of honor, among other things, that pertained among the Romans, including the self-imposed sanctions attendant upon rape in time of war—not in an ambiguous situation in a boudoir. War is a public activity. So is wartime rape. It is not a private act. By deconstructing codes that sustained a woman's destruction by her own hand given this public violation, Augustine offers an alternative public evaluation and code: rape in wartime is what violators do to the violated. That is the assumption with which one begins. There is no requirement that the woman restore her honor as her honor has not been undermined in the eyes of the new community—it is the perpetrator who has dishonored himself.

49. DCD, Book II, chapter 2, p. 49.

50. Ibid., Book III, chapter 21, p. 122.

51. Here I refer the reader to the extended discussion in *Women and War*, chapter 4.

52. DCD, Book XIV, chapter 13, p. 571.

53. DCD, Book X, chapter 28, p. 413.

54. Ibid., p. 415.

55. *The Confessions*, Book VIII, p. 168.

56. DCD, Book XX, chapter 21, p. 939.

3. Against the Pridefulness of Philosophy

1. Augustine, *Select Letters*, no. 49, pp. 386–87.

2. Ibid., p. 385.

3. Brown, "Political Society," pp. 320–21.

4. Augustine, *Selected Writings*, Homilies on the Psalms, "Psalm 122: God Is True Wealth," p. 250.

5. This has been much noted by a variety of Augustinian scholars, some with rue; others with raves.

6. I do not intend to go into Augustine's often pained reasoning about the ultimate fate of unbaptized infants. He has frequently been

excoriated for dooming them. For me, this is not a central issue for the purpose of this book and, I daresay, not really a central issue for our time in a political sense. It is, of course, a big issue for the devout. I myself come from a family of the baptized. Remembering one's baptism is a memory that structures much of the recognition of limits and openness to new possibility that Augustine would have us be about.

7. DCD, Book XIV, chapter 9, p. 565.

8. Ibid., Book XIX, chapter 4, p. 855.

9. The Confessions, Book I, chapter 8, p. 29.

10. Augustine, Select Letters, no. 2, p. 7.

11. Ibid., no. 22, p. 147.

12. The Trinity, Book One, chapter 1, p. 4. Hereafter DT.

13. DCD, Book XVI, chapter 32, pp. 693–94.

14. Ibid., Book XI, chapter 26, p. 460. Although we are alone in our ability to attain "real knowledge" of a certain sort, according to Augustine, we are not alone in our "wish to exist." "Why, even the irrational animals, from the immense dragons down to the tiniest worms, who are not endowed with the capacity to think on those matters, show that they wish to exist and to avoid extinction. They show this by taking every possible action to escape destruction." (DCD, Book XI, chapter 27, p. 461.)

15. Ibid., Book XIX, chapter 6, p. 860.

16. Charles Norris Cochrane, Christianity and Classical Culture (New York: Galaxy Book, 1959), p. 396–97.

17. Michael André Berstein writes brilliantly of the raw destructiveness that emerges when form is destroyed, exposing, as he does so, the bien pensant utopianism behind contemporary celebrations of the carnivalesque. See Bitter Carnival: Ressentiment and the Abject Hero (Princeton: Princeton University Press, 1992).

18. Cochrane, p. 384.

19. James Wetzel, Augustine and the Limits of Virtue (Cambridge: Cambridge University Press, 1992), p. 15.

20. A point made repeatedly and eloquently by Cochrane: vicissitudo spatiorum temporalium.

21. Augustine, Select Letters, no. 46, p. 351.

22. Wetzel, Augustine and the Limits of Virtue, pp. 8, 10.

23. Augustine, Select Letters, no. 41, p. 317. As is always the case with

Augustine, he is intent on preserving a complex tension between works and grace, and he chastises those who go too far in the other direction, so to speak, and create the opposite of the Pelagian dilemma by "extolling grace to such an extent that they deny the freedom of the human will" (*Select Letters*, no. 50, p. 305).

24. DT, Book Three, Preface, p. 95.

25. Ibid., Book One, chapter 3, pp. 8–9. What these many men share in common is faith, but faith does not guarantee identical texts.

26. Ibid., Book I, chapter 10, pp. 27–28.

27. Ibid., chapter 31, p. 47.

28. Ibid., Book Five, chapter 9, p. 187.

29. Ibid., chapter 12, p. 191.

30. Ibid., Book Seven, chapter 2, p. 219. And what is ineffable will vary from language to language. See Augustine's comments on Greek and Latin and the way essence and substance are variously expressed. (Ibid., chapter 4, p. 229.)

31. Ibid., chapter 12, p. 241.

32. Pope John Paul II, "Apostolic Letter on Augustine of Hippo," *Origins* 16, no. 16 (October 2, 1986), 284.

33. Augustine much preferred the scientists to the superstition of the Manichees. Scientists have discovered much. But this also puts them in the danger zone as they are easily flattered and "their conceit soars like a bird." *The Confessions*, Book V, p. 93.

34. DT., Book Three, chapter 11, p. 120.

35. Ibid., Book Four, chapter 1, p. 131.

36. Augustine, *Select Letters*, no. 10, p. 89.

37. DT, Book Eight, chapter 6, p. 257.

38. Augustine, *Select Writings*, Homilies on the Gospel of St. John, First Homily, p. 278.

39. The title, of course, of John Paul II's encyclical on truth.

40. Augustine, DT, Book Ten, chapter 2, p. 294.

41. Ibid., Book Ten, chapter 8, p. 305.

42. A free interpolation of DT, Book Ten, chapter 11, p. 311.

43. Ibid., Book Eleven, chapter 4, pp. 324–25.

44. Ibid., chapter 8, p. 336.

45. Ibid., Book Ten, chapter 14, p. 308.

46. DCD, Book XI, chapter 27, pp. 461–62.

47. Ibid., chapter 28, p. 462.

48. Ibid., pp. 462–63.

49. Ibid., Book XXII, chapter 24, p. 1075.

50. Ibid., Book XXI, chapter 3, p. 966. Pain is also a harbinger of things to come, the perpetual life in pain and torment of the condemned. This foreshadowing many will, and can, reject without simultaneously rejecting the fact that pain signifies life.

51. Ibid., Book XIV, chapter 13, p. 572.

52. See *The Confessions*, Book VII, for this story, esp. pp. 164–65.

53. Ibid., p. 214. If this sounds a bit Freudian, it should. I am convinced that Freud did a lot more than just dip into Augustine for his own philosophy of mind, but that is another story.

54. This is a rough summation of part of the discussion in *The Confessions*, Book X, one of the most extraordinary texts, or chapters of a text, in the story of Western thought. There is such delight and wonder in reading it, one cannot help but be beguiled by its author, who has become a problem to himself.

55. Ibid., p. 224.

56. DCD, Book XV, chapter 26, p. 643.

57. *The Confessions*, Book IX, chapter 5, p. 189.

58. DCD, Book XI, chapter 28, p. 413.

59. Ibid., chapter 29, p. 415. By "then or now" my primary reference point is to humbling, whether the agent of that humbling is the Cross or some other.

60. Dennis Martin, "In the Form of a Servant: Trinitarian Victimization and Critical Hermeneutics," unpubl. ms., p. 2.

61. Ibid., pp. 3–4.

62. DT, Book Thirteen, chapter 17, p. 401. It should be noted that Augustine insists that the Devil will "get his," so to speak, because, being disembodied, although he cannot be tormented in time, he can be tormented in eternity. Because the Devil doesn't suffer death of the flesh, he has become "inordinately proud. . . ." But just wait, "another kind of death is prepared in the eternal fire of hell, by which not only the spirits with earthly bodies, but also those with aerial bodies can be tortured." Ibid., Book Four, chapter 13, p. 154. We don't go in for this sort of thing anymore, although we still torture real human beings all the time.

63. *Select Letters*, no. 55, p. 475.

4. Augustine's Evil, Arendt's Eichmann

1. Albert Camus, "The Human Crisis," *Twice a Year*, 1946–47, pp. 20–21.

2. Ibid., p. 22.

3. Ibid., p. 23.

4. Ibid., p. 24.

5. Hannah Arendt, *The Origins of Totalitarianism* (New York: Harvest Book, 1973), p. ix. George Kateb reminds us that her description of the death camps as "an absolute evil" appears in the preface to *Origins*, including the second edition, but this is omitted from the three-volume edition. For Kateb, the preface is somewhat anomalous, given Arendt's overall analysis of totalitarianism. See George Kateb, *Hannah Arendt: Politics, Conscience, and Evil* (London: Martin Robertson, 1984), p. 54.

6. Arendt, *The Origins of Totalitarianism*, p. 5.

7. Ibid., p. 479. The Augustine quote is from DCD, Book XII, chapter 21, although Arendt cites chapter 20.

8. Hannah Arendt, *Eichmann in Jerusalem: A Report on the Banality of Evil* (New York: Penguin Books, 1964).

9. Arendt notes, with deep sarcasm, that Eichmann simultaneously proclaims himself no *Gottgläubiger*, "to express in common Nazi fashion that he was no Christian and did not believe in life after death. He then proceeded: 'After a short while, gentlemen, *we shall all meet again.*'" (Arendt, *Eichmann*, p. 252.) Arendt can scarcely conceal her contempt.

10. Ibid., p. 136.

11. Ibid., p. 252.

12. Kateb, *Arendt*, p. 74.

13. Ibid., p. 288.

14. Cited in Kateb from an interview Arendt did with the *New York Review of Books*, p. 79. The *New Yorker* magazine recently rediscovered evil in the form of Hitler. The author, Ron Rosenbaum, "Explaining Hitler" (May 1, 1995, pp. 50–70), writes of the "magnitude" of Hitler's evil, proclaiming him something of an evil genius who defies ordinary explanation. The terms "radical evil" reemerge in full force. The text is accompanied by six photographs of Hitler from 1927, "taken while he rehearsed gestures to a recording of one of his speeches." Of course, they are riveting. The evil genius is restored and reborn once again.

15. Arendt, *Eichmann*, p. 276. See Christopher Browning's chilling account, *Ordinary Men: Reserve Police Battalion 101 and the Final Solution in Poland* (New York: Harper Perennial, 1992), for an account of how average, middle-aged Germans turned ugly and how evil too easily became routine.

16. "'Eichmann in Jerusalem,' An Exchange of Letters between Gershom Scholem and Hannah Arendt," *Notes and Topics* 22 (January 1967), p. 56.

17. William S. Babcock, "Augustine on Sin and Moral Agency," *Journal of Religious Ethics* 16, no. 1, (Spring 1988), pp. 28–55, is a fascinating attempt to unpack Augustine on sin and the free exercise of will.

18. *The Confessions*, p. 53.

19. I assume that the neoplatonic backdrop to Augustine's changing views on evil and his critique of Manicheanism is too well known to comment on here. My interest is with what Augustine does with the neoplatonic understanding, given his acceptance of the Christian story of creation and the story of Christ's birth, life, suffering, and redemption—the Incarnation.

20. *The Confessions*, Book II, chapter 7, p. 63.

21. DCD, Book IV, chapter 12, p. 152.

22. *The Confessions*, p. 13.

23. Ibid., Book V, chapter 10, p. 103.

24. Ibid., Book V, p. 105.

25. Ibid., Book VII, chapter 2, p. 135.

26. For contemporary treatment of this theme, see Milan Kundera, *Unbearable Lightness of Being* (New York: Harper and Row, 1984), especially the story of the circle dance.

27. DCD, Book VIII, chapter 25, p. 337.

28. Ibid., Book XI, chapter 9, p. 440.

29. Ibid., chapter 15, p. 446.

30. Ibid., chapter 17, p. 448.

31. Ibid., chapter 18, p. 449.

32. Ibid., XII, chapter 7, p. 479.

33. Ibid., Book XI, chapter 22, p. 454.

34. Ibid., Book XII, chapter 4, p. 474.

35. Ibid., Book XIV, chapter 11, p. 569.

36. Ibid., Book XI, chapter 23, p. 454.

37. Arthur Cohen, *An Admirable Woman* (Boston: David R. Godine, 1983), p. 94.

38. Arendt, *Eichmann in Jerusalem*, p. 233.

39. See Kateb's discussion, although we are really making different sorts of points, in *Arendt*, pp. 55–56.

40. Ibid., p. 81.

41. Philip Hallie, *Lest Innocent Blood Be Shed*, (New York: Harper Colophon, 1980).

42. Hannah Arendt, *The Life of the Mind* (New York: Harcourt Brace Jovanovich, 1978), p. 4.

5. "Our business within this common mortal life": Augustine and a Politics of Limits

1. Brown, "Political Society," p. 317, citing from Augustine, *Sermon* 169, p. 14.

2. Brown is eloquent on these matters. See especially his chapter on Augustine and the Pelagians in *Augustine of Hippo*.

3. Augustine, *Letters*, no. 44, p. 343.

4. Cited in Brown, *Augustine of Hippo*, p. 375.

5. John Neville Figgis, *The Political Aspects of S. Augustine's City of God*, in his discussion of Book XVIII.

6. R. A. Markus, *Saeculum: History and Society in the Theology of St. Augustine*, (Cambridge: Cambridge University Press, 1970) pp. 35, 42.

7. Ibid., pp. 98, 103.

8. Milbank, *Theology and Social Theory*, p. 389.

9. Ibid.

10. Milbank discusses this, as does Augustine himself, of course, in deflating the claims of Rome. But it goes much beyond Rome to a general discourse on human societies.

11. Milbank makes this point, as I do in *Women and War*.

12. Augustine, DCD, Book XIV, chapter 1, p. 547.

13. Ibid., Book XV, chapter 27, p. 648.

14. Ibid., Book XIX, chapter 6, p. 860.

15. Ibid., chapter 13, p. 872.

16. Ibid., chapter 14, p. 873.

17. Ibid., Book XIX, chapter 18, p. 878.

18. Ibid., chapter 20, p. 880. Interestingly, we now have empirical evidence that those who are regular churchgoers and participants are more deeply involved in serving their neighbors and in being trustworthy and reliable than those who are not thus involved. See the recent work of Robert Putnam.

19. DCD, Book XIX, chapter 21, p. 881.

20. Ibid., chapters 23 and 24, p. 890.

21. Markus, *Saeculum*, p. 146.

22. In a way Markus really makes this point himself in his discussion of the remarkable similarity in Bonhoeffer's and Augustine's treatments of the ultimate and the penultimate (the *saeculum*). See ibid., p. 172 ff.

23. Ibid., p. 168, 170. Bonhoeffer's great works include *The Letters and Papers from Prison* and *The Ethics*.

24. Milbank, *Theology and Social Theory*, p. 403.

25. Ibid., p. 405.

26. Ibid., p. 409.

27. Ibid., pp. 417–18.

28. Ibid., p. 420.

29. Ibid., p. 421.

30. See, for example, her conclusion of *The Origins of Totalitarianism*, p. 479.

31. DCD, Book XII, chapter 22, p. 502.

32. Ibid.

33. DCD, Book XIV, chapter 1, p. 547.

34. Ibid., Book XV, chapter 16, p. 623.

35. Ibid., chapter 16, p. 624.

36. Ibid., p. 625.

37. Ibid., Book XXI, chapter 8, pp. 981–82.

38. See Markus and the distinction between Augustine's 'here and now' and the Donatist's 'within/without' and the importance of this distinction.

39. Brown, "Political Society," pp. 322–23.

40. All these are cites from my discussion of Augustine in *Women and War* (New York: Basic Books, 1987), p. 130. The key Augustinian discussion on war is, of course, DCD, Book XIX. But his deconstruction of the

Roman 'Pax' takes place throughout all of Part I, Books I-X. See, for example, DCD, Book IV, chapter 15.

41. Again, all drawn from *Women and War*, p. 130.

42. Milbank, *Theology and Social Theory*, p. 390.

43. Ibid., p. 391.

44. Williams, "Politics and the Soul," p. 62.

45. See my *Democracy on Trial* for further elaboration on this theme. (New York: Basic Books, 1995.)

46. DCD, Book XVII, chapter 13, pp. 743–44.

47. Ibid., Book XIX, chapter 7, pp. 861–62.

48. Ibid., chapter 12, pp. 866–67.

49. Ibid., pp. 867–68.

50. Michael Loriaux, "The Realists and Saint Augustine: Skepticism, Psychology, and Moral Action in International Relations Thought," *International Studies Quarterly* 36 (1992), pp. 401–20.

51. Ibid., p. 408.

52. DCD, Book XIX, chapter 11, p. 866.

Epilogue: Loving Crazy Horse and Augustine

1. Augustine, *Select Letters*, no. 42, p. 329.

2. Ibid., no. 8, p. 49. In another letter, Augustine argues against vengeance in these words: "it is not our desire that the sufferings of God's servants shall be avenged by the infliction of similar punishments, as if by way of retaliation; not that we refuse to allow wicked men to be deprived of impunity in crime, but that we rather desire that justice be satisfied in such a way as to turn the wicked by means of coercive measures from their mad frenzy to the peaceableness of sane men, without taking their life or crippling them in any part of the body, and so set them to some useful work instead of their works of malice." (Letter no. 34, p. 253.)

3. Hannah Arendt, *On Violence* (New York: Harvest HBJ, 1970), p. 35.

4. Ibid., p. 56.

5. Ibid., p. 20.

6. Albert Camus, *The Rebel* (New York: Vintage Books, 1956), p. 234.

7. Ian Frazier, *The Great Plains* (New York: Farrar Straus Giroux, 1989), pp. 117–19.

8. DCD, Book X, chapter 14, p. 392.

9. Ibid., p. 588.

10. Ibid., Book XXI, chapter 5, pp. 969–70.

11. Ibid., Book XXII, chapter 30, p. 1091.

12. DT, Book 3, p. 96.

Although the primary source for this work has been primary sources, I have learned much from but a few among that vast—frighteningly vast—number who have delivered up tomes and comments on Augustine of Hippo. A few should be mentioned. Some have been cited in notes; others have not. I have learned from and been provoked by all. Frederick Copleston, S.J., Ernest Fortin, William Babcock, Peter Brown, Rowan Williams, Robert Markus, Romand Coles, George Kateb, Margaret Miles, John Milbank, William Connolly, Joanna Scott, Gilbert Meilaender, James Wetzel, Peter Bathory, Joshua Mitchell, Stanley Hauerwas, Glenn Tinder, Charles Norris Cochrane, Henry Chadwick, Gareth Matthews, Richard Neuhaus, Hannah Arendt, and Pope John Paul II. I beg the reader's indulgence, and the scholar's forgiveness, for those I have encountered over the years but have, at least for the moment, forgotten.

INDEX

absolute sovereignty, 100, 114
Addams, Jane, 97–98
Admirable Woman, An (Cohen), 84–85
affections, human bonds of, 102–3
affirmation, 55, 91
aggression, 107. *See also* war
allegory, use by Augustine, 51, 95, 97, 99
angels, 83; bad/fallen, 58, 81, 83, 95
"Apostolic Letter on Augustine of Hippo" (John Paul II), 57
Arendt, Hannah, 1, 6, 71–77, 81, 84–85, 101; *Eichmann in Jerusalem*, 72–76, 85; *Life of the Mind*, 86–87; *Origins of Totalitarianism*, 71–72, 127n5; *On Violence*, 114
assent, necessary for sin, 76
astrologers, faith in criticized, 7
auctoritas, 10. *See also* authority
"Augustine as Narcissist" (Capps), 9–10
Augustine of Hippo, 2–4, 113–15, 116–18; Camus's dissertation on, 71; influence on Arendt, 72, 76–77. *See also* City of God, The; Confessions; Trinity, The
authority, 2, 5, 21, 40, 99; of the Church, 26; in the *civitas*, 34, 40; crisis of, 17

bad (fallen) angels, 58, 81, 83, 95
Bakan, David, 9
banality of evil, 73–77, 81, 84–87
baptism, 123–24n6
beauty, 57–58, 61–62, 82
beginning as supreme capacity of man, 72, 101
being, 11, 18, 63, 89
Berstein, Michael André, 124n17
biologism, intrusion into political thought, 114
body, 11, 81, 95, 96, 99; epistemic significance, 54–55, 58, 60; received from a woman, 46, 65
Bonhoeffer, Dietrich, 98, 130nn22, 23
Brown, Peter, 3, 4–5, 15, 42, 61, 105; on *The City of God*, 24–25; on dependence on others, 50
bureaucracy, growth of, 70

Camus, Albert, 69–71, 115
Capps, Donald, 9–10
caritas, 50, 89; ethic of, 36–37, 38–42, 55–56, 91
categorical imperative, Kantian, 72–73
categories, 14, 54
charity. *See caritas*
choice, 55, 80, 82

135